D1138035

"Our world is made up of those who make things ha[...]
The leaders and the led. And what makes the differe[...]
know how to persuade. I ha[...] ne[...] [...]e[...] [...]nyone
Bounds. And in th[...] [...] [...]ow yo[...] [...]an acquire it."

Drayton Bird, the [...] [...]eac[...]g [...]rity on direct [...]keting

"Another excellent book from Andy Bounds, designed to help businesses communicate more effectively. Ours is one of the world's largest accounting networks, and over the last 12 months Andy has transformed the way we speak with our clients, prospects and colleagues. His techniques and methods are simple but effective, and they are making a big difference to our business."

Geoff Barnes, CEO and President, Baker Tilly International

"Yet again, Andy Bounds provides us all with effective, quick to use and impactful advice and techniques. In today's and the future business environment, where everything is online, 140 characters, and sometimes even face-to-face, communication is everything. Making each of these interactions outstanding for the other person marks you out as someone different. With Andy and this book as our guide, we can become better communicators, step-by-step."

Paul Patterson, Sales & Marketing Executive Director, Fujitsu

"I've seen the great impact this book's techniques can have. My colleagues have embraced Andy Bounds' advice, and are communicating better than ever before – both with each other and with our customers."

Matthew Dunn, Sales Director, Data & Analytics, Experian Marketing Services

"Andy Bounds is one of the most insightful and inspirational global business experts. His ideas transform companies. Having seen the impact he has on an audience, and having met managers who have benefited from his ideas, I am in no doubt that *The Snowball Effect* should be required reading for anyone who wants to see their business thrive."

Alan Stevens FPSA, PSAE, Past President, Global Speakers Federation

"A must-read book! In today's fully global, fast-paced society, communication underpins everything people do and effective communication is crucial for success in both business and in life. This is the essential, practical, easy-to-read guide that will revolutionize the way you communicate in order to get more done and do it more quickly, more pleasantly, and less stressfully for optimum results in all that you do."

Ivan Misner, Ph.D., NY Times Bestselling Author and Founder of BNI®

"The impact that Andy's advice has on people is, quite simply, stunning. Andy's techniques are easy to implement; more importantly, they deliver results. I guarantee anyone will pick up new ideas from his book. Even better, new ideas they can use the second they put the book down. *The Snowball Effect* isn't a nice-to-have; it's a must-have book. Buy it, read it and reap the rewards."

Aberdeenshire

[...] of *Do It! or Ditch It*
[...]oaching Academy

3098637

The Snowball EFFECT

Communication Techniques to Make You Unstoppable

Andy Bounds

CAPSTONE

Library of Congress Cataloging-in-Publication Data is available

A catalogue record for this book is available from the British Library.

ISBN 978-0-857-08397-5 (pbk) ISBN 978-0-857-08398-2 (ebk)
ISBN 978-0-857-08400-2 (ebk) ISBN 978-0-857-08399-9 (ebk)

Set in 10/12 pt Myriad Pro Light by Toppan Best-set Premedia Limited
Printed in Great Britain by TJ International Ltd, Padstow, Cornwall, UK

To Em, Meg, Jack, Maia and Tom –
My angels and my demons x

Contents

Introduction

Imagine how life-changing it would be if your communications suddenly became better than everyone else's.

The benefits would be huge. After all, great communicators are more successful. They get more done. They persuade others more easily. They enjoy their jobs more.

So, there you go. It's as simple as that. Just communicate better, and you'll achieve great things.

The problem, of course, is that it isn't "simple" to communicate brilliantly. If it was, your diary wouldn't be full of tedious conference calls, pointless meetings, and presentations where you watch somebody read out their slides.

And also, it's taken you your entire life to develop your current communication style. It's part of you. And it's hard to break such entrenched habits (after all, how many "transformational" workshops have you attended that changed things for 1–2 days only, if that?)

THE ONLY WAY TO IMPROVE YOUR COMMUNICATION SKILLS FOREVER

I've helped some of the world's largest companies to communicate better. I've spoken at conferences in 30+ countries about communication best practices. My mum is blind, so I've a lifetime's experience of talking to someone who can't see things the way I do – an essential skill when communicating. My previous book *The*

Jelly Effect: How to make your communication stick is an international bestseller (it was only kept off the Amazon #1 spot by the final *Harry Potter* book).

So, I know how to help people make long-lasting improvements to how they communicate. And one thing I've seen again and again is:

> **The best way to improve forever is to keep adding simple techniques, embedding them as you go.**

The alternative – trying to change loads of things at once – always ends with people reverting back. It's like how detox diets always lead to retox binges.

This means that making a *permanent* change is like building a snowball: you make the core, then roll it down the hill, adding new layers as you go.

This book will help you build your snowball. I'll show you simple techniques to help you communicate better than ever before. This is something people often find hard to do, for all sorts of reasons:

- They communicate in the order they think. This means that their main points – the ones that required most thought – appear towards the end. But their audience's concentration reduces during their communications. So by the time they reach their main points, people have switched off.
- They prepare by thinking "what do I want to say?" not "what do I want them to *do* after I've said it?". But communication is supposed to *cause* something. That's the point of it. So, their first thought should always be to identify its purpose, then work backwards to decide what needs to be said to achieve it.
- They expect others to follow their thought processes, by showing how to get from Startpoint A to Conclusion Z. But what if the audience is starting at point B instead? A Londoner wouldn't direct a New Yorker by saying "starting in London, you . . ." because the other person isn't starting there.

HOW *THE SNOWBALL EFFECT* WILL IMPROVE YOUR COMMUNICATION

The book has five sections:

- A   **Build Your Core: The Cornerstone of Successful Communication**
- B   **Get More Done More Quickly: How to Save One Month per Year**
- C   **Persuade More People to Say "Yes": How to Convince Others to Do What You Want**

D   Enjoy Your Job More: How to Make Work More Fun
E   Eliminate the Negatives: How to Remove Your Communication Frustrations

These contain lots of short chapters, each showing a simple technique you can use the minute you finish reading. If you like, each chapter is a new bit of snow to add onto your core.

The chapter titles show what each technique will help you achieve. You can read them in whichever order you want – each makes sense on its own. So:

If you want to...	The best way to read the book is to...
Find out how to communicate in a certain situation.	Read the chapter titles and go straight to the relevant one(s).
Learn everything about a particular aspect of communication, e.g. effective meetings.	Look in the Index for all the pages that relate to meetings.
Read it as a book.	Go cover-to-cover!

Whichever you choose, I advise you start with **Section A – Build Your Core: The Cornerstone of Successful Communication**. This shows how to build a solid foundation. It helps you create your snowball's core. Get this right and you can build a brilliant snowball. Miss it out and the snow has nothing to stick to.

THIS BOOK IS A GREAT START. BUT IT'S ONLY A START

This book will make a big difference to you. Apply the techniques and you *will* communicate better.

But it's only a start. As Irish author George Bernard Shaw said: "The single biggest problem with communication is the illusion that it has taken place." In other words, people think communication's finished. But it often isn't. It needs constant, rigorous, disciplined reinforcement and follow-up.

And, just as communication never ends, neither does learning how to master it. So, to help embed this book's techniques: test them, use them, then adapt them to suit your situation.

Let's be honest: it isn't easy to communicate perfectly.

But it *is* easy to make small changes that lead to huge improvements.

And, the better you do this, the more unstoppable your snowball becomes.

Andy Bounds
January 2013

SECTION A

Build your core

The cornerstone of successful communication

This section only contains one chapter. But it's the most important one. It underpins *everything* in the book.

In this chapter, you'll learn how to master the three steps of preparing communication. You'll see:

- These three steps are much more likely to work than what you do now.
- It's easier to use them than it is to keep doing what you currently do.
- They're very different to what practically everybody else does, so using them is a great way for you to stand out.

Once you've mastered them, you've built your snowball's core. You can then roll it through the book, picking up new techniques as you go.

SECTION A

Build your core

The cornerstone of successful communication

1

How to prepare communication that works

Great people get things *done*.

This means their communications must cause others to *do* things.

However, most communication isn't like this. Instead of causing the *do*, it transfers understanding:

- Let's *share* the new strategy, *inform* everyone of the company's vision, *update* each other, *upskill* the team.
- During today's meeting, we will *discuss* A, B, C.
- The *content* of my presentation is X, Y, Z.

But transferring understanding only *tells* people things. You want your communications to *cause* something. That's the point of them. They're a means to an end, not the end. In fact, my Golden Rule of Communication is:

> **Communication is only effective if it causes the DO.**

In other words, the only way to tell whether a communication has worked is by what the recipients *do* as a result. For example, a strategy roll-out is only effective if people change their behaviours. A workshop is only effective if delegates' performance improves. An email is only effective if the reader does what you want.

It sounds so obvious. But people don't think of this as often as they should, focusing instead on what they want to talk about. After all, how many:

- Meetings go on too long and achieve nothing?
- Presentations leave you thinking, "OK, I get it. But what am I supposed to do now?"
- Conference calls make you think, "Well, that was a wasted hour I'll never get back."

So, with communication, it's not what you *say*, it's what you *cause*. After all, which meeting would you rather attend? One starting with "Today's meeting will last 60 minutes, and the agenda is A, B, C, D and E", or "The purpose of this meeting is to help us *do* X and Y. As soon as we can, we'll finish".

THE PROBLEM WITH HOW PEOPLE PREPARE COMMUNICATION

Communication has three elements – the start, content, and end. And people usually prepare in that order – the start, then the content, then the end:

- With emails – they write the title first, then line 1, then lines 2, 3 . . .
- With presentations – slide 1, then slides 2, 3 . . .
- With meetings/conference calls – agenda item 1, then items 2, 3 . . .

And this approach makes sense. After all, it's the order in which the points will be discussed.

But, even though it's the most widespread approach, it isn't the best. Far from it. And here's why.

Someone recently asked for my feedback on this email:

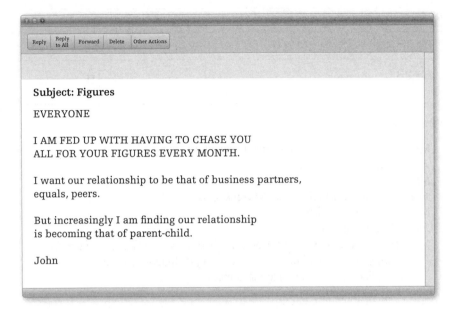

Subject: Figures

EVERYONE

I AM FED UP WITH HAVING TO CHASE YOU
ALL FOR YOUR FIGURES EVERY MONTH.

I want our relationship to be that of business partners,
equals, peers.

But increasingly I am finding our relationship
is becoming that of parent-child.

John

There's clearly a lot wrong here! It's rude, abrupt, and impersonal. The capitals suggest shouting. It probably should have been a phone call instead.

But there's a bigger problem. John didn't ask the readers to *do* anything. So they didn't. He broke the Golden Rule about the DO.

You see, one of the problems of preparing communications in the traditional "start–content–end" way is that, like John, people often forget to add the DO at the end. To remedy this, they need a better approach to communicating.

THE 231 APPROACH: THE BEST WAY TO COMMUNICATE EFFECTIVELY

Since the DO is the most important thing – after all, it's the reason you're communicating – your first step must be to start there.

Step 1: Start with the end (the DO)

	Start	Content	End
Traditional	1st	2nd	3rd
The 231 Approach			1st (DO)

When John showed me his email, we had this chat:

Me: So, what did you want people to *do* after reading it?
John: *Send me their figures.*
Me: I bet they didn't, did they?
John: *They didn't actually. How did you know?*
Me: You didn't ask them to.
John: *Well it's obvious.*
Me: Not to me. And, even if it was, I didn't know *which* figures; or *how* you wanted me to send them; or by *when*. I just thought you were shouting at me and calling me childish.

There are three steps to creating a clear DO:

1. Make it very specific, by asking yourself "What–When–How":
   What: Send me this month's figures.
   When: By the end of the week.
   How: By email.
   (Note: you don't address "why" here. As you'll see shortly, this goes in the title.)
2. Introduce it pleasantly – "Please can you" is more likely to work than "I need you to".
3. Give them context – and therefore motivation – by adding what you'll do with their DO:
   In John's case, this was that, after receiving their figures, he'd input them into his system.

The bottom of John's email now reads as:

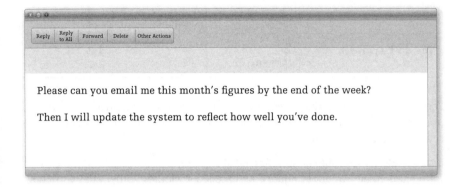

> Reply | Reply to All | Forward | Delete | Other Actions
>
> Please can you email me this month's figures by the end of the week?
>
> Then I will update the system to reflect how well you've done.

Pretty clear, yes? And much more likely to work.

And, of course, this "DO step" isn't just for emails:

- When the last slide of your presentation says "Thank you", your audience will say "You're welcome". Nice, but not the only impact you wanted. However, when the slide says "Next steps", there tend to be some.
- In meetings, when you start with the agenda, people focus on the agenda. But when you start with the meeting's *purpose* – the DO – everyone focuses on that. So more gets done, and in much less time.
- When writing a document, adding a box which says "Action required" on the front gets quicker, better responses.

Here's one final tip about the DO: in John's example, his team had to do their DO (send the figures) *before* John could do his (put them on the system). Sometimes, *your* action isn't dependent on people doing *theirs* first. When this happens, go first. Research shows when you give first, people usually feel they "owe" you, so are more inclined to reciprocate quickly.

So, starting with the DO is a great start. But there are two problems with it as it stands:

1. There's no benefit to his team of doing the DO. If it's not in their interest to do it, they won't want to do it; and
2. John's email is called "Figures" – a boring title that means the email mightn't even be opened.

The second step removes both problems.

Step 2: Create an intriguing title/intro (using AFTERs)

	Start	Content	End
The **231** Approach	**2**nd (AFTERs)		**1**st (DO)

Your title/intro should draw people in. Your email titles should mean they get opened. Your Slide 1 should make people want to see Slide 2. Your meeting titles should ensure people attend.

Unfortunately, most titles simply *describe* the content. This is what happened with John – the email was about figures, so he called it "Figures". Other titles you'll have seen/heard thousands of times include "Update", "Miscellaneous", "Q2 Overview", "Our background/process/expertise". And, of course, good old "FYI".

Don't all these sound *boring*?

To create intriguing titles/intros, use something I call AFTERs: explain why they'll be better off *AFTER* hearing you (so, this is where you address the "why" question I mentioned earlier).

AFTERs are great for securing buy-in. They're what people always want. For instance, nobody buys toothpaste because they want *toothpaste*; they want clean teeth AFTER using it. Nobody wants a hairbrush; they want nice hair. Nobody wants a newspaper; they want the news. And *nobody* wants an email called "Figures".

In John's example, the recipients' figures had a direct bearing on how much they got paid. This gave him the title:

> **"Making sure you get paid the right amount this month."**

You can imagine how quickly people responded to this, compared to "Figures"!

And again, this step applies to all communication, not just emails:

- Always include the main AFTER in either the title (like John did), or a subtitle – "Excel Intermediate: *How to save a day every month*".
- Where appropriate, reinforce it with your introductory sentence – "This communication will help us to [AFTER]".
- And, if you're writing a business book, don't just call it *The Snowball Effect*! On its own, it doesn't make sense. It's much better to put an AFTER in the subtitle: *Communication techniques to make you unstoppable*.

Some people think it feels odd to say the *why* before the *what*. But it's important to say the *why* first. It instantly switches the recipient's brain from apathetic to engaged, so they then receive your communication more positively.

This works pretty well at home too. For example, if I say to my children, "Please will you go to bed", they start thinking "no" the minute they hear the word "bed". In fact, they're so pre-occupied with the loathsome word "bed" that they don't listen to the AFTER I might have added "and I'll give you a million pounds".

But flip it round, start with the AFTER, and look what happens:

Me: Hey kids, do you want a million pounds?
Them: Yes please, Dad.
Me: OK. All you have to do is go to bed.
Them: Great. I'm going now.

It's pretty expensive, but it sure does work!

One final (but very important) note about AFTERs: they can either be business related ("this will help you reduce costs") or emotional ("this will help you feel part of the team"). As you know, people often decide based on emotion, and then justify based on logic. So, make sure your AFTERs tie into what *really* drives the person you're speaking with.

So the rule is: state their AFTER *first*, not *after* everything else.

Step 3: Write your content (minimum length; maximum interest)
And finally – at last! – we get to the content.

	Start	Content	End
The **231** Approach	**2**nd (AFTERs)	**3**rd (minimum length; maximum interest)	**1**st (DO)

So far, the first two steps have shown:

1.   *What* you want them to do.
2.   *Why* they'll benefit after doing so.

There's often not much more to say. Look at John's email now:

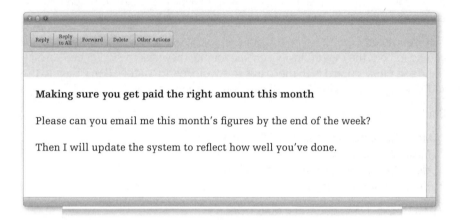

Making sure you get paid the right amount this month

Please can you email me this month's figures by the end of the week?

Then I will update the system to reflect how well you've done.

He probably only needs to add "Hi there" at the top, and "Best wishes, John" at the bottom, and it's complete.

Of course, you'll usually need to add more content than that. But the good news is that your content only has to satisfy two criteria:

1. Minimum length: keep asking "Do I really need to include this, if all I want is for them to do Step 1's DO?"; and
2. Maximum interest: make it as interesting as possible – use humour, good visuals, stories, interactivity, and so on.

I cover both – in lots of detail – elsewhere in the book.

HOW TO KNOW YOUR COMMUNICATION HAS WORKED

Obviously, one measure of success is "did they do the DO?" In other words, John could say his email worked if they all sent him their figures.

And, for such a simple communication, that's success. But, with longer, more involved communications, there's a bit more to it. After all, you want to *engage* people, not just *tell* them what to DO.

My four criteria for successful communications are that:

1. It worked – you got the result you wanted. They did the DO.
2. You liked delivering it. When you enjoy something, you're more likely to deliver it with passion, positivity and persuasiveness.
3. Your recipient(s) liked receiving it. This means they're more likely to buy-in and agree more quickly.
4. It was as short as possible.

It's easiest to remember these by thinking WITS:

Worked
I liked it
They liked it
Short

When you achieve all four, it's a great communication.

If any are missing, it could've been better.

If *all* are missing, it couldn't have been much worse.

Given this, you'll know you've succeeded when you trigger all four.

	How to do it	Questions to ask yourself
Worked	Being clear on your DO. Remove flabby content that bulks things up, but adds nothing.	*"What content could I strip out <u>without</u> harming my chances of it working?"*
I liked it	Include elements *you'll* enjoy.	*"How can I make this more engaging for <u>me</u>?"*
They liked it	Include elements *they'll* enjoy.	*"How can I make this more engaging for <u>them</u>?"*
Short	Edit aggressively, removing as much as possible.	*"What else can I do, to shorten this?"*

The rest of this book has one aim: to help you be *brilliant* at achieving all four, every time you communicate.

FOCUS ON 231, NOT 123

So, the three steps of successful communication are:

	Start	Content	End
You *prepare* in this order	**2**nd (AFTERs)	**3**rd (minimum length; maximum duration)	**1**st (DO)
You *speak* in this order	**1**st	**2**nd	**3**rd

The benefits of using this technique are *huge*: better conversations; shorter, more interesting conference calls and meetings; presentations that work; emails that people reply to. It's just a better way to communicate.

In fact, its only "weakness" is that some people think it sounds so obvious – basic, even – that they presume they do it more than they do.

But everyone's so busy now, rushing from one thing to the next, that "obvious things" don't always happen. Bad habits become the norm.

For instance, one of my customers, Julie – an organizational effectiveness expert in the financial services industry – told me this story, which I imagine will feel pretty familiar to you:

In my first week of an international assignment, my MD was worried that an imminent management conference was going to be a train wreck.

We chatted about what he wanted the conference to achieve for his business, and about why he felt it wasn't going to happen. He then asked me to listen in on a Meeting Planners' conference call.

But, when I did, it was *terrible*. They just kept going round in circles. For example, they spent ages discussing how to cram a two-day coaching workshop into two hours. It just wasn't going to work.

So, I put on my "231 hat" and asked what they wanted delegates to <u>do</u> differently after the conference.

Silence.

In fact, it went so quiet that I wondered whether I'd offended my new colleagues!

Fortunately, I hadn't. But, as I probed more, they realized they didn't know what the managers needed, and had guessed "coaching" was the answer.

Our conversation uncovered that the actual problem was that managers weren't feeding back in ways that improved performance. So, we changed the agenda to focus on that.

And it worked brilliantly. For the first time in years, the managers enjoyed the conference. Even better, their teams told us they loved receiving the new feedback, even when it was "developmental"!

When I reflected on this call, in many ways, it felt like we hadn't made much of a change – all we'd done was stop focusing on the day, and start focusing on what they'd do after it.

But, then I thought again. This one tiny tweak had transformed <u>everything</u>.

TWO FINAL THINGS TO HELP EMBED THE 231 APPROACH

Firstly, to help you prepare all future communications, here's this chapter's content in a simple template:

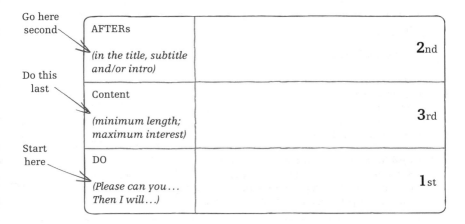

Go here second

AFTERs

(in the title, subtitle and/or intro)

2nd

Do this last

Content

(minimum length; maximum interest)

3rd

Start here

DO

(Please can you ... Then I will ...)

1st

And secondly, to see how your different communications – presentations, emails etc. – might look, turn to the Templates appendix at the back of the book.

NEXT STEPS – IN OTHER WORDS, YOUR "DO"

Now that you know the three 231 steps, here are a few things to do:

- Use 231 on a short, simple communication today; and/or
- Identify an important communication you've got coming up, and apply 231 to it; and
- Now that you've built your core, add snow to it by learning techniques to help you communicate better in specific situations. Why not go to the section that's most relevant to you (note the sections' AFTERs titles!):

   Section B – Get More Done, More Quickly: How to Save One Month per Year
   Section C – Persuade More People to Say "Yes": How to Convince Others to Do What You Want
   Section D – Enjoy Your Job More: How to Make Work More Fun
   Section E – Eliminate the Negatives: How to Remove Your Communication Frustrations

Build Your Core: Prepare Communication that Works

To communicate more effectively, prepare in a different order to how you speak.

You speak in the order:

- Start first
- Content second
- End third

But prepare in the order:

- End first – what you want them to *do*.
- Start second – why they'll be better off AFTER doing it.
- Content third – keep it short and interesting: what's the minimum you need to say, to convince them to do it?

SECTION B

Get more done more quickly

How to save one month per year

WHY THIS MATTERS

Communication takes too long, doesn't it?

In fact, a recent McKinsey study found people spend only 39% of their week doing the day job (in other words, that's three days per week doing "other stuff". What a waste of time).

I've spent many years helping "unblock" companies' communication. It makes a huge difference – you should see what it does to people's engagement and productivity.

In the same way, you can "unblock" *your* communication, to give yourself lots more time. In fact, saving just one minute per day equates to four hours per year.*

So, to get an extra month (approximately 200 hours) per year, you "only" need to free up 50 minutes a day.

That sounds a lot. But this section will show you how to do it. Each chapter contains a time-saving technique. Simply write your savings at the end of each chapter. Then, total your savings, and see if you've saved a month.

It's a great target to have. I mean, even if you spectacularly "failed" and *only* freed up a fortnight per year . . . well, you've just freed up a fortnight per year.

And what a *boring* fortnight it would've been.

---

*If you care, here's the rationale: you work approximately 240 days per year (48 weeks × 5 days). There are 60 minutes in an hour. Therefore, to find annual hours, multiply daily minutes by 240/60 i.e. by 4. So 1 minute per day equates to 4 hours per year.

2

When you want to ensure people do what you want immediately

Imagine you have only two things on your To Do List:

TO DO LIST

1. *Buy bread.*
2. *Restructure finances.*

Which is more important? (The finances)

Which would you do first? (The bread)

Why? Well, one reason is because it's unclear how to start with the finances. After all, the first step of buying bread is obvious – go to the shop and buy it. But the first step of restructuring your finances?

When you want to do something, you need to know where to start. In other words, you need total clarity on your *first step*.

And, this is also critical when you're giving actions to others. After all, when people don't act on what you say, it can look like resistance or defiance. But it's more often due to them not knowing what to do, and/or how to start. Being crystal clear with their first step removes this problem instantly.

But, unfortunately, people's Calls To Action are often just rallying calls – "Restructure your finances!", "Improve teamwork!", "Sell more!", "Increase engagement!" and the like. All have one thing in common: the recipients could well think, "I know that. I want to do it. But how do I go about it?"

STEP 1: IDENTIFY *WHAT* THE FIRST STEP IS

Since people need to know where to start, prepare by working backwards: begin with your rallying call and keep saying "Before that" until you get to the first step:

Restructure my finances
Before that, go to the bank
Before that, make an appointment with someone at the bank
Before that, know who that someone is
Before that, call the bank, ask them who to speak to and book an appointment
Before that, find the bank's telephone number
Before that, go to telephone directory (so this is the *first step*)

STEP 2: BE CLEAR *WHEN* YOU'LL DO THIS FIRST STEP

You know to look in the telephone directory first but, without a deadline, there's no urgency. So, this second step is – although important – very simple: just add a deadline – "I'll look up the number in the telephone directory *after work today*."

STEP 3: ENSURE YOU REMEMBER, BY REMINDING YOURSELF

Even if you know exactly *what* to do, and *when* to do it, you could still forget to do it, because it didn't pop into your head at the right time (let's face it, we've all experienced this before). So do something to remind yourself – for example, put a reminder in your diary or ask someone to remind you.

So, let's look at your To Do List now:

TO DO LIST

1. Buy bread.
2. Look up the bank's number in the telephone directory after work today (reminder's in the diary).
3. Call the bank tomorrow morning, ask who I need to speak with and set up an appointment (also in diary).

This three-step process means it's now as easy to start the finances as it is to buy bread. This makes it much more likely to happen.

And it's the same when giving actions to others. Be clear on their first steps and deadlines, plus offer to help them remember.

So, for the other rallying calls I mentioned earlier, you might say instead:

Rallying call	Call to Action
Improve teamwork	"Starting next week, please call each other at least once every week, and arrange a time to meet. I've diarized to call in a couple of weeks, to see how it's going."
Sell more	"Please go to your customer list, and identify the people who've previously bought a lot from you. Then, call them and say, 'X'." "I'd like you to do this some time this week. I've put it on next week's agenda, so you can each feed back how you did."
Increase engagement	"Please change your team meeting agenda by inserting a new item to discuss every month: 'How can we improve engagement with our colleagues?' The first meeting this will impact is next week's."

This is a great technique for triggering instant action, but you need time and head-space to think about it. The next chapter shows you how to get a lot more of this than you have now.

Build Your Snowball: Ensure People Do What You Want Immediately

To ensure people do your Calls To Action right first time:

1. Clearly identify *what* the first step is ("Pick up the phone" not "Restructure finances").
2. Be clear *when* they'll do this first step.
3. Help them remember, e.g. diary reminders or you call them.

This technique could save me _____ minutes per day.

×4

This would equate to _____ hours per year.

3

When you want to find the time to communicate brilliantly

Time is never about time. It's about *priority*.

In other words, there's always the time you need to communicate brilliantly. The question is whether it's a high priority for you, compared to everything else that's going on.

If you *do* think it's important, it will need to feature prominently in your Priority Place – the place where you list your important actions. This will, I guess, be your diary or To-Do List.

And you'll often get quicker, better results if you put *three* reminders in your Priority Place, not *one*. Let me explain.

HOW TO FIND THE TIME YOU NEED

Important communications have three elements: the preparation, delivery and follow-up.

However, people often only put one or two of these in the diary, that is, the delivery (and sometimes the preparation).

But this means you have to fit the follow-up (and, if you haven't diarized it, the preparation) around your priorities in your diary. In my experience, this results in people:

- Prepping at home at the last minute (or not doing any at all).
- Not following-up well (or ever).

This reduces your chances of a good outcome:

- Poor preparation often leads to poor communication.
- Zero follow-up often leads to zero action.

Admittedly, preparation and follow-up take time. But nowhere near as much as you'll spend chasing up a communication that didn't work. So, to prioritize your pre/post work, use three diary entries:

1. Put "Preparation" in the diary, at a time when (a) your brain is at its best (morning?) and (b) you're unlikely to bump it in favor of other priorities.
2. Diarize your delivery as you usually would (the techniques in this book – especially this section – will reduce the time you need for this, since your communications will be much shorter).
3. Diarize "Follow-up" *immediately* after the delivery. This could well only be a five-minute diary entry, but it helps you roll the "momentum snowball" you wanted your communication to initiate. This follow-up could be as simple as a standard email that you tailor to each situation, something like:

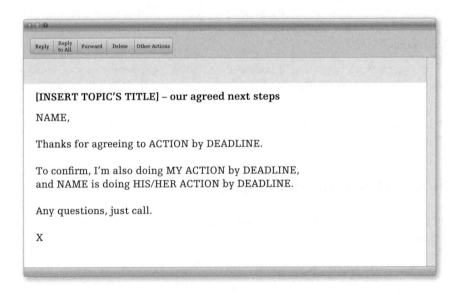

One final thought about this chapter: it assumes you're in control and that you've the time to free up more time for preparation/follow-up.

Sometimes, the world's not like this and you find yourself having to deliver important communications with *zero* preparation time. The next chapter shows a very effective way to do this.

Build Your Snowball: Find the Time to Communicate Brilliantly

To make sure you have the time you need, insert three diary entries, not one:

1. Preparation.
2. Delivery.
3. Follow-up (to take place immediately after the delivery).

And, if you think people might need chasing up, add a fourth: to chase them up!

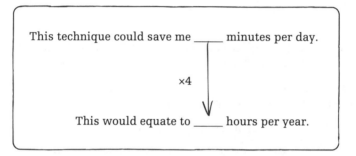

This technique could save me _____ minutes per day.

×4

This would equate to _____ hours per year.

4

When you want to impress senior audiences when you haven't much time

Some communications are career-defining. Amaze your audience and you may never look back; underwhelm them and you may never recover.

Presentations to senior audiences can be like that. You want to impress them. You certainly won't want to come out with any regrets.

But this isn't always easy to do. Especially if this happens:

> "The agenda's over-run, so we're going to have to shrink your 30-minute presentation down to five. What did you want to say?"

Recognize this? It happens pretty frequently, doesn't it?

But, if you want to impress them, you *have* to react impressively. And people don't always. For instance, some reactions I've seen – **but do *not* endorse** – are:

- Deliver the same content six times more quickly.
  This just ends up a mess.
- Give handouts and say "please turn to page 8".
  They don't. They flick through the pack and don't listen to you.
- Offer to come back another day.
  This *might* work. But how do you know things won't over-run then? And, how do you know you'll be a priority to them? If you aren't, you won't even get on the agenda.

No, a better option is to present using the four steps "Wallop–Down–Up–Please":

1. **Wallop:** start with a big bang (often this will be showing the impact of *not* changing – the rationale: people buy to avoid pain).

2. **Down:** make this impact worse.
3. **Up:** show you have an alternative which will improve things.
4. **Please:** ask them to do something.

For example:

> Thanks for your time today.
>
> We are needlessly wasting £230,000 per month on X (Wallop).
>
> Even worse, this number will increase over the next couple of months. Projected needless waste will cost £2.8 million this year. This will increase to over £5.6 million in the next couple of years (Down).
>
> We can reduce these costs by over 75% – that's a potential saving of over £4 million – by implementing X [spend 2–3 minutes explaining your proposal] (Up).
>
> Therefore, given that successful implementation could deliver £4 million of savings, please can I ask you to do Action X (Please).

See how this works? You grab their attention immediately. Your message is impossible to ignore. You stand out from other presenters (who, let's face it, probably had a first slide saying "Background" or some such).

An added bonus: you get instant, positive feedback, in that you can tell it's worked because they:

- Agree to your request; and/or
- Show interest and ask questions; and/or
- Give you longer than 5 minutes!

WHY WALLOPING IS A TIME-SAVING TIP

When I wrote this chapter, I wasn't sure whether to put it in the next section "Persuade More People to Say 'Yes'" or this one "Get More Done More Quickly".

It could have been either. But, in the end, I chose here because I wanted to reinforce the huge time savings that this approach brings. It takes only minutes to do, which is much quicker than traditional preparation. In fact, a number of my customers *always* use Walloping as their first "preparation step" because:

- It quickly gives clarity on key issues.
- They can present their "Wallop version" as is, if appropriate; or can use it to help shape their next iteration.

- It guides them on impactful visuals. For instance, in the above example:
  - The first visual could be a slide which only had one thing on it – "Needless cost: £230,000".
  - A click would change this number to £2,800,000.
  - The next click would change this number to £5,600,000.
  - The next click would replace all those words with "Saving £4,000,000".

Or, of course, you could simply just deliver the same content six times faster!

Walloping's great for when you want to make a big impact very quickly. Sometimes though, your aim will be to make a *permanent* impact. This requires a different technique, which I cover in the next chapter.

Build Your Snowball: Impress Senior Audiences, When You Haven't Much Time

Prepare two presentations – your traditional one, plus a "Wallop–Down–Up–Please" version.

- Wallop – a big bang start, showing the negatives of *not* changing.
- Down – make the negatives worse.
- Up – offer a solution to remove this now-big negative.
- Please – ask them to act.

This is very quick to prepare, and gives you a great option if you need it.

This technique could save me _____ minutes per day.

×4

This would equate to _____ hours per year.

5

When you want to ensure people remember your key messages

Walt Disney used to say that his theme parks needed a "weenie" – iconic landmarks to draw visitors in – like Cinderella's Castle at the Magic Kingdom, or the Tree of Life at Animal Kingdom ("weenies" being the sizzling sausages that entice you towards a hotdog stand). If you've been to any Disney park, you'll know how eye-catching their weenies are.

Similarly, when you're communicating, you'll sometimes have one key message – your weenie – you want people to hear and act on. You want it to stand out amongst all your other messages, so it causes an instant, dramatic, and *lasting* impact on everyone who hears it.

There are lots of techniques to help draw attention to your weenie:

1. **Unclutter content:** Strip out everything you can, apart from your weenie. You'll have plenty of other opportunities to mention them.
2. **Say it early:** People's concentration dips during a communication, so say your weenie *early*. Then continually reinforce it. Don't build up to saying it at the end, as your audience might have switched off by then.
3. **Introduce it, so they know it's key:** Use "definite" words to introduce it, so they know it's important: "There's only one thing I want you to focus on this year, which is . . . ".
4. **Reinforce your weenie, by highlighting the problems of *not* changing:** Say what you *don't* want people to do: "If we don't change and keep doing X, Y will happen".
5. **Be clear on the changes people must make:** If your weenie means people have to act differently, say so. To ensure they understand what

they're changing from and to, start by referring to what they do now: "Whereas you're currently doing X, I now want you to do Y instead".

6. **Give crystal clear Calls To Action (maybe using "for instance"):** You want to eliminate the chances of people *not* doing what you want. For example, if your weenie/key message was "please enhance our reputation", even if everyone remembered the message, they wouldn't necessarily know what to do about it.

    Using "for instance" makes it much easier for them: "So, going forward, I want you to enhance our division's reputation within the company. *For instance*, you could:
    - Call your key contacts, and ask how we can help them more.
    - Think what's been well received in the past, and do it again.
    - Ask colleagues how they've enhanced their reputation, and copy it.
    - Identify other divisions that impress you, and learn from them".

7. **Repeat your weenie during your communication:** There's lots of research discussing how often people need to hear something before it sticks. Recommendations vary, but they all agree people need to hear things *more than once*.

    So, repeat your weenie. Say it in different ways. Enhance it with examples, stories, visuals, analogies, and the like.

8. **Repeat your weenie *after* your communication:** Use follow-up communications to reinforce your key message. Ask your managers to mention it in all their team meetings. Give the "unofficial leaders" – the ones you need to get on side when you want to change things – the responsibility and motivation to keep mentioning it for you.

When you have one weenie, do all you can to get your message across (if you've more than one message, the next chapter shows you how to communicate them all). The key thing to remember is your audience has lots on their minds, not just your weenie. So help make it impossible for them to forget.

Build Your Snowball: Ensure People Remember Your Key Messages

To quickly ensure people remember your one key message (your "weenie"):

• Unclutter content.
• Say it early.
• Introduce it, so they know it's key.
• Reinforce your weenie by highlighting the problems of *not* changing.
• Be clear on the changes people must make.
• Give clear Calls To Action.
• Repeat it in different ways during your communication.
• Repeat it after your communication.

Some of the techniques in this book provide a choice of options. I'll often end by saying "do the ones you think are best for you".

But this one's different. If you want your key messages to stick, there's a strong argument for you doing *all* of the above to help people remember.

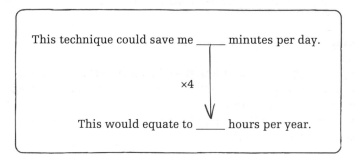

This technique could save me _____ minutes per day.

×4

This would equate to _____ hours per year.

6

When you want to quickly create presentations that work

Let's face it, most presentations aren't that good. Too long. Too many wordy slides. Too little interaction. Too dull.

And, when you look at how people prepare, you can see why. Do you recognize any of these?

- Seeing what slides you currently have, and trying to base your content round that.
- Leaping straight to PowerPoint, rather than thinking first.
- Using the same presentation that you recently delivered to somebody else, whether it worked or not.
- Delegating 100% of the preparation to someone else, and hoping they give you exactly what you want.

All these are definitively quick. But, this speed is often a false economy, since the *slowest* thing about communication is when it *doesn't* work. So, it's worth investing more time upfront.

This chapter shows a simple technique to make your presentations stand out from the crowd – always a good thing. It's also a great time-saver in two ways:

1. It's quicker to prepare.
2. It's more likely to work first time.

The technique builds on **Section A: Build Your Core – The Cornerstone of Successful Communication**. So, if you've not read that yet/recently, you might want to do so first. Anyway, here goes.

THE FIVE STEPS OF CREATING A GREAT PRESENTATION

Successful presentations have five elements that – in effect – work down your audience's body.

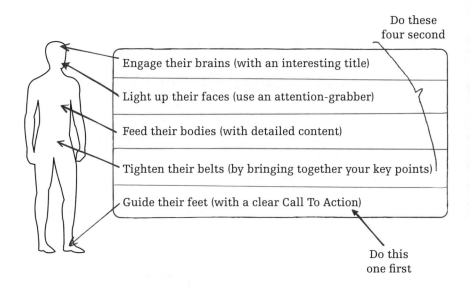

Do these
four second

Engage their brains (with an interesting title)

Light up their faces (use an attention-grabber)

Feed their bodies (with detailed content)

Tighten their belts (by bringing together your key points)

Guide their feet (with a clear Call To Action)

Do this
one first

Step 1: Guide their feet (with a clear Call To Action)

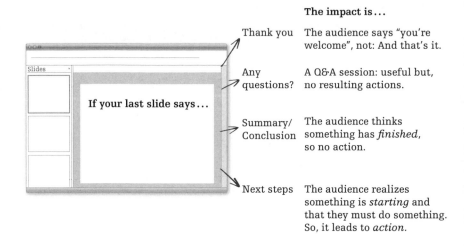

The impact is...

If your last slide says...

Thank you — The audience says "you're welcome", not: And that's it.

Any questions? — A Q&A session: useful but, no resulting actions.

Summary/ Conclusion — The audience thinks something has *finished*, so no action.

Next steps — The audience realizes something is *starting* and that they must do something. So, it leads to *action*.

So, if you want your audience's feet to move – in other words, that they *do* something – you'll have to:

1.   Tell them they need to move; and
2.   In which direction.

Two approaches that work well:

Approach 1: Show you're doing something too

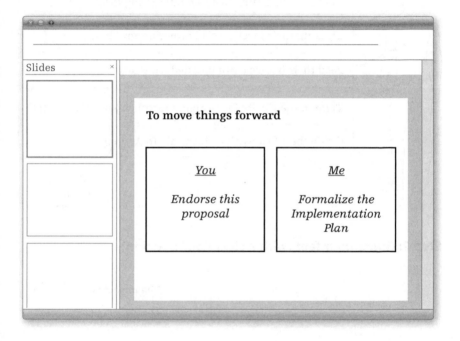

Approach 2: Give them options, so they choose the actions

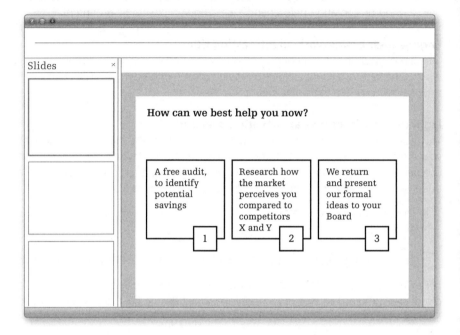

Both approaches are very effective. I've used the first to help deliver results like secure multi-million-pound budgets, resolve long-lying problems, and help people get promoted. It's also very effective when you have more actions than your audience – it makes it harder to say "no".

The second version – where you give options – also moves the audience's feet, because it empowers them to choose the next step.

For instance, one of my customers – a multinational telecoms company – used to deliver credentials presentations to new contacts with the last slide saying "Thank you". This triggered zero next steps.

So, I rewrote their last slide to the one above and every presentation now triggers a next step. The customer either chooses one of the options, or says "I'm not sure about these three, but how about doing X instead?"

Step 2: Write the content
You could write the world's best last slide but it's only going to work if you've delivered a good presentation beforehand. Here's how to create great content.

Engage their brains (with an interesting title)
The aim of your first sentence is that they want to hear your second one: "Update" won't achieve this; "How we can increase employee engagement" will. Chapter 25 shows how to create titles that draw people in.

Light up their faces (use an attention-grabber)
You want to grab your audience's attention right from the start. This means it's *your* – not their – responsibility to get it. There are various techniques that you can use here – all of which will be familiar to you. It's just a question of choosing the one(s) that will make *this* audience really sit up. For instance, you could use:

- Thought-provoking questions.
- A new opinion.
- Humour.
- An interesting fact (a good way to introduce it is to say "Did you know?").

For example, I used a combination of these at a recent sales conference where I'd discovered beforehand that most people felt "relationship building" was the key to increasing sales.

> Good morning everyone. Did you know that the Sales Executive Council recently found that only 7% of superstar salespeople are relationship-builders? The rest do something quite different.

In just three sentences, everyone was listening.

Feed their bodies (with detailed content)
It's now time to write your content. The two rules with content are that it should be (a) interesting and (b) short. The quickest way to do this is:

1. Write your skeleton. This will be your presentation's (very) few main points. These will act as your chapter headings.
2. Flesh out each chapter, remembering "maximum interest; minimum duration".
3. Lay out your content as follows:

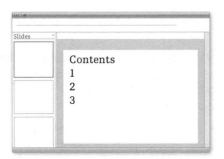

A contents slide, showing the chapter headings only, so they "get" the flow. This slide also appears later (see "belt-tightening" below)

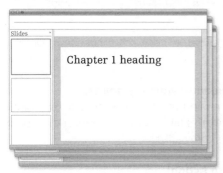

All Chapter 1's slides, the first being a "title slide" to highlight the chapter's start

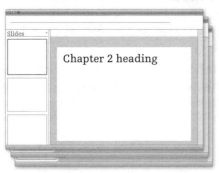

The same for Chapter 2

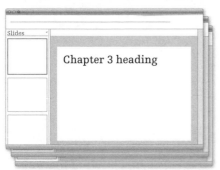

And Chapter 3

Structure is critical. Your audience (and you!) want to know where you're taking them.

A good illustration: Drayton Bird is widely regarded as the world's leading authority on direct marketing. His book *Commonsense Direct and Digital Marketing* has been continuously in print for 30 years and is published in 17 languages; his clients range from The Royal Mint to Peppa Pig. He once told me:

> "You taught me to organize my talks far better – to signpost and tell them what they would get; remind them where we were up to as I went through my (usually very long) seminars; then remind them at the end what I had promised.
>
> Before you, I delivered inspirational rants; now, I deliver organized inspirational rants."

Tighten their belts (by bringing together your key points)
After you've delivered your content, remind the audience of your key points by showing them the contents slide again. This takes about three seconds to prepare – you simply copy and paste the slide from earlier.

Guide their feet (with a clear Call to Action)
Now that you've delivered your presentation, it's time to ask them to move their feet by showing the Call to Action slide you created first. And, let's face it, if the previous steps went well, this one will.

Presentations are a big source of frustration in business (as are meetings – check out the next few chapters for how to deal with them). But preparing in this way gives you a much better chance of achieving your twin aims of (a) succeeding (b) quickly.

Build Your Snowball: Quickly Create Presentations That Work

To create an impactful presentation, work down their body

1. Engage their brains (with an interesting title).
2. Light up their faces (use an attention-grabber).
3. Feed their bodies (with detailed content).
4. Tighten their belts (by bringing together your key points).
5. Guide their feet (with a clear Call To Action).

Prepare in the order 5, 1, 2, 3, 4, in that the Call To Action must drive the content, not the other way round.

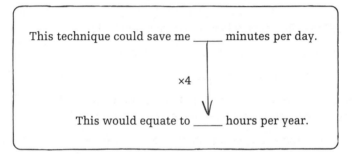

This technique could save me _____ minutes per day.

×4

This would equate to _____ hours per year.

7

When you want to have better, quicker meetings and conference calls

In theory, all meetings should help you do your job better.

In theory, they should help you make better decisions.

In theory, they should speed things up.

The reality is, of course, very different. In fact, just as we've all heard the phrase "Death by PowerPoint", I'm surprised there isn't a similar one: "Inertia by meetings".

When you think about it, meetings should be like pit-stops in a Formula One race:

- They help you win.
- They're fast and energetic.
- Everyone who's there needs to be there.
- Lots of pre-work means the meeting is hyper-efficient.
- They're action/improvement-focused.
- Things would be worse if you didn't have them.

Instead, they're often more like being forced to have Huge Sandwich Breaks while you're busy:

- They interrupt what you'd prefer to be doing instead.
- They're big and bloating.
- There's only so many you can have before you start to work with less energy and focus.
- You didn't choose them. In fact, you'd choose *not* to have them.
- 99% of them are totally forgettable, even though they were expensive.
- Worst of all: they make your day worse.

And do you know the weirdest thing of all? You know these meetings that people hate? Well, they organize some of them themselves.

One way to ensure your meetings are shorter and more interesting is to agree a set of guidelines that you'll all follow. If you want universal buy-in, the key word here is "agree", not "impose" (though you might end up with better guidelines if you suggest something and invite comment).

Examples I've seen work well include:

Meeting guidelines

1. Our meetings are short pit-stops (energized refuels that help us win), not sandwich breaks (bloating interruptions that slow us down).
2. The meeting is more important than you. If you can't contribute, haven't done the preparation or the agenda isn't a priority for you, please don't come.
3. When you're the decision's owner, only call a meeting if you need one. Wherever possible, make the decision yourself or through 121 discussions.
4. If you do need to hold a meeting:
   Formulate your ideas, and circulate to all attendees beforehand, telling us exactly what you want us to do with them. In other words, don't come unprepared, expecting us to "create by committee".
   Be open to people's suggestions for improvement to your pre-reads.
   Review all presentations/material that people want to bring before the meeting. It's your responsibility to ensure they're interesting/appropriate to discuss at your meeting.
   Only invite people who can contribute. Don't waste others' time.
   Only book the time you need for the decision. Don't just insert a standard 30- or 60- minute time slot.
   And, if in doubt, make it shorter.
5. If you've been invited to a meeting, but can only contribute to part of the agenda, and ask in advance for your items to be discussed first. Then, after we've discussed them, please feel free to leave.
6. For meetings that are under 10 minutes long, stand up don't sit down.

Good points, yes? So, either use them all or – if it's too many for people to remember – choose a few, and then make them memorable, say by making their initial letters spell a word, like PALM (see chapter 9).

As long as they improve your meeting, everyone agrees with them and – critically – *follows* them, guidelines are essential in ensuring consistently high standards.

All the above guidelines work well. They're so useful that I'm going to expand on a few of them in the next couple of chapters. I'll start by addressing the biggest time-waster of all: how to get out of meetings you don't want to go to.

Build Your Snowball: Have Better, Quicker Meetings and Conference Calls

Agree meeting guidelines that you all commit to following.

To create these guidelines, take inspiration from other groups who achieve great things when working together, like pit-stop crews.

It's also worth reviewing the guidelines every 2–3 months, asking:

- Are we still doing all these?
- Which guidelines should we change?
- How can we help each other improve our meetings?

This technique could save me _____ minutes per day.

×4

This would equate to _____ hours per year.

8

When you want to only attend the meetings you need to

When people get invited to meetings, they often act as if their options are:

- Option 1 – go to the meeting.

And that's it.

You're invited, so you have to go, right?

Well, not exactly. It's a meeting invitation, not a court summons. When you're invited, you actually have three options:

- Option 1 – go to the meeting.
- Option 2 – *not* go to the meeting.
- Option 3 – go, but in a different way than the invite suggests.

Ignoring the third for now (we'll come back to it later – it's very useful), here are some questions to help decide between the first two – whether to attend or not:

1. Is the meeting covering something you can contribute to, feel passionate about and/or will be involved in implementing afterwards? (If it is, you should probably go.)
2. If you didn't go, but received a copy of the resulting actions, would that be enough for you? (If it would, you probably shouldn't go.)
3. If you didn't go, will "Somebody Important" think badly of you? (If they will/might, you should probably go. Or at least speak to them before declining.)
4. Is it symbolically important you're there? (If it is, you should probably go.)

You'll notice the word "probably" appears a lot. That's because the personalities and politics involved mean there are no absolute do/don't rules. But if you decide *not* to go, tell the owner beforehand, saying "Thanks for inviting me", followed by something like:

- "Looking at the agenda, I think it's best I don't come. You'll have lots of strong opinions on this, and mine aren't as important."; or
- "I don't think I can contribute much to this agenda, so won't attend."

If appropriate, you can always add "Please send me a copy of everyone's actions, so I know what's happening next".

So, we've covered the first two options – whether to attend or not. Let's now revisit the third – to attend the meeting, but in a different way. Here are a few examples you could consider, alongside what to say to help them happen.

Alternative to attending	Type of thing you might say
Dial in, rather than attending in person.	"I'm not around that day, but am happy to dial in. What's the best number for me to call?"
Attend some of the meeting, but not all.	"I can only contribute to agenda items 3 and 6. Would you mind putting them at the beginning, so I can come just for them?"
Send someone in your place.	"I'm keen that my team's involved, but this is more Tom's area than mine. So, he'll attend in my place."
Meet 121 with the owner before the meeting.	"I'm afraid I can't attend the meeting, but I have some ideas that will help. How shall I get them to you before the meeting? Email? Or should we grab a coffee?"

By the way, if you're dialing in, here's a quick tip.

Have you noticed how there can be long silences in conference calls?

One reason is that, without visual cues, people don't know when it's their turn to speak. My mum – who, as a blind person, knows a lot about this – first pointed this out to me. I've since found it to be true. And it makes sense: if you went to a meeting where everyone had their eyes shut, it would be much harder for people to speak up.

So, when you're dialing in – or, indeed for any conference call – remember it's like you're meeting with blind people. There are no visual cues. So, instead:

- Use people's names, so they know you're talking to them.
- When you speak, start with your name, so they know it's you "It's Andy. My thoughts on this are . . ."
- Ask more closed questions – they're easier for people to answer. You can always ask a follow-up open question to the person who responded to the closed one.

And here's two important points to finish.

Firstly, just as this section's techniques will help you with meetings that *others* organize, so too do they help others with meetings that *you* organize:

- If someone doesn't need to be there, don't invite them (though consider sending the resulting actions to them afterwards).
- If someone could be there but in a different way – dial-in, attend the first part only etc. – ask which they'd prefer.

And secondly, when people attend your meetings, make them *brilliant* (or why would they attend future ones?). The next chapter teaches you a simple way to do this, using my PALM technique.

Build Your Snowball: Only Attend the Meetings You Need To

When you're invited to a meeting:

- Accept if it will help you (or cause you problems if you don't).
- Decline if you're not needed (it's OK to send your apologies in advance).
- "Accept" (often the best) but in a different way, for example:
  - Dial-in
  - Attend the first bit only
  - Send someone in your place
  - Meet 121 with the owner
  - Ask to be copied in on actions

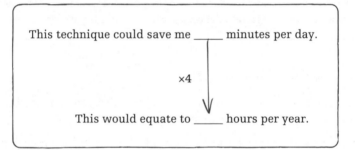

This technique could save me _____ minutes per day.

×4

This would equate to _____ hours per year.

9

When you want to prepare for meetings in the right way

Have you noticed how most agendas contain too many topics that make things take longer than they should?

When people prepare for meetings by starting with the agenda, it means they're only thinking about what to *discuss*, not what they want to *achieve*. And, because it's easy to find a reason to discuss pretty much any topic, this makes the agenda too long and full of non-essentials.

Instead, a much better approach is to prepare using PALM:

Purpose	What you want to achieve as a result of the meeting.
Agenda	The decisions you need to make at the meeting, to ensure you achieve this **P**urpose (note: "decisions to make", not "discussions to have").
Limit	The maximum time you'll allow for this **A**genda.
Minimum number of attendees	The less people there, the better. After all, you want to optimize, not compromise. Deciding by committee is *never* efficient.

And you need all four:

Without the **P**, you don't know your end-point. And, as American psychologist David Campbell said:

"If you don't know where you're going, you'll end up somewhere else."

Without the **A**, there's not enough structure. The meeting becomes a free-for-all.

Without the **L**, meetings overrun and/or are needlessly long. After all, when you say a meeting will last an hour, it does. But when you say it will last "a maximum of an hour", it's often less.

Without the **M**, decisions take longer. And while it might seem a good idea to invite more people, look at the increased number of agreements this means you need:

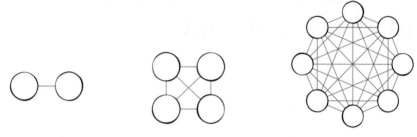

2 people = 1 agreement   4 people = 6 agreements   8 people = 28 agreements

(And if you drew one for 16 people, it would take 120 agreements!)

A PALM meeting's agenda looks like this:

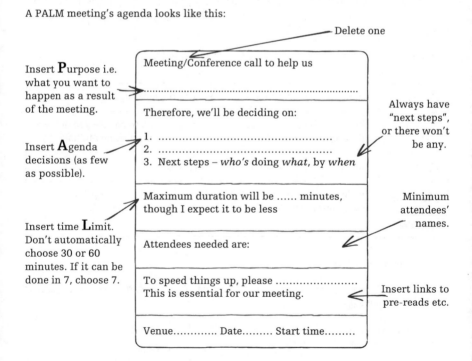

Delete one

Insert **P**urpose i.e. what you want to happen as a result of the meeting.

Meeting/Conference call to help us

....

Therefore, we'll be deciding on:

Always have "next steps", or there won't be any.

Insert **A**genda decisions (as few as possible).

1. ....
2. ....
3. Next steps – *who's* doing *what*, by *when*

Maximum duration will be ...... minutes, though I expect it to be less

Minimum attendees' names.

Insert time **L**imit. Don't automatically choose 30 or 60 minutes. If it can be done in 7, choose 7.

Attendees needed are:

To speed things up, please ....
This is essential for our meeting.

Insert links to pre-reads etc.

Venue............. Date......... Start time.........

So, an example would be:

Conference call to help us
identify an easier way to hit target

Therefore, we'll be deciding on:

1. *Which option(s) we should pursue*
   (see attached)
2. *Our Top Tips for injecting pace*
3. Next steps – *who*'s doing *what*, by *when*

Maximum duration will be *15* minutes,
though I expect it to be less

Attendees needed are: Anna, Emma, Peter and Jo

To speed things up, please read the attached
options and call me to discuss (or bring your
proposed improvements to the meeting). Also,
think about your Top Tip for injecting pace.

Both are essential for our meeting.

Venue *Jo's office* Date *Tues 12th* Start time *9.15am*

You can see why this works:

- It's set up to be an output-focused, fast pit-stop; not an indigestible, bloated break.
- It helps ensure the meeting generates actions (the next chapter has more on this).
- People prepare for it better. Did you notice the comment about the pre-reads: "essential for our meeting". You're adults having a professional work meeting, not schoolchildren having a chat. People need to respect other attendees' time, and do the pre-work. I've seen people make this point in different ways – one that sticks out is, "If you don't prepare, don't come". So, choose your own approach, but be clear that preparation is a must-do, not a do-if-you-want.

Build Your Snowball: Prepare for Meetings in the Right Way

Think PALM:

Purpose – What do you want the meeting to achieve? (Note: "achieve" not "discuss".)

Agenda – What decisions need to be made, to achieve the purpose? (Note: "decisions", not "discussions topics".)

Limit – What's the maximum time you'll allow? (Note: not "this will last 60 minutes because that fits nicely in my Outlook diary".)

Minimum – What's the *smallest* number of people we need there? (Note: not "who else can we invite?")

This technique could save me _____ minutes per day.

×4

This would equate to _____ hours per year.

10

When you want to ensure meetings generate actions, not just discussion topics

Some meetings are little more than glorified chats. Lots discussed, but not one action arising. These are a drain on your time – especially if they happen every week. Team updates, anyone?

To resolve this, you can:

- Keep the content the same, or change it; and/or
- Keep the duration the same, shorten it, or just stop having the meeting.

In my experience, the worst option is usually to keep both content and duration the same. After all:

- If you waste *an hour* every week at meetings like this, stopping them would save you *one week* per year (to remind yourself how I worked this out, please see this section's introduction).
- Therefore, if these meetings involve say 26 people, stopping them would free up 26 working weeks – that's half an employee! – for no cost or hassle. Even better, none of you would have to waste time in this rubbish meeting any more.

TURNING DISCUSSIONS INTO ACTIONS

You might well still want/need to meet for at least some time. So, to make things more effective, identify how to take *less* time to trigger *more* actions.

Here's one simple solution: after every discussion topic, ask questions to identify the action to take, focusing on three key elements – *who's* doing *what*, by *when*. For example:

- Who:
  - "Which of us should take an action, to move this forward?"
  - "Who's responsible for progressing this?"
- What:
  - "What action should we take as a result of this conversation?"
  - "What are our next steps here?"
- When:
  - "What's the deadline for this action?"
  - "When do you want to update us on your progress?"

You'll notice these questions don't appear much in update meetings. That's one reason they can be so dull, pointless and an unrelenting drain on your time. The next chapter shows how to transform these into action-generating sessions.

But with updates – or indeed *any* meeting – unless you ask questions like these, people won't be clear on their actions.

And, when actions aren't clear, they don't happen.

MAKING SUCCESS INEVITABLE

However, even if you *are* clear on your actions, they *still* might not happen. Work sure does have a habit of getting in the way.

So document the actions (what's happening next) – not the minutes (what was discussed) – and send a follow-up email. Something like:

| Reply | Reply to All | Forward | Delete | Other Actions |

Agreed actions following our INSERT TITLE meeting on INSERT DATE

Hi there,

Thanks for your time at the meeting.

To confirm, these are our agreed next steps:

What (action)	Who (name)	When (deadline)

Thanks in advance for completing your actions.

If you have any questions, please contact NAME on CONTACT DETAILS.

Regards,

Tips like this really work. I was recently discussing "Meetings" with one of my customers, Debbie Harrison (Debbie specializes in learning, leadership and talent development, and has helped some of the world's largest companies revolutionize their people's abilities and motivation). She's used my techniques to overhaul how various companies conduct their meetings. She told me it *always* improves things, the main benefits being:

1. Meetings consistently achieve the desired outcome.
2. Less wasted time.
3. More productivity.
4. Better engagement.
5. Increased job satisfaction (by removing something people used to hate).

**Build Your Snowball: Ensure Meetings Generate
Actions, not just Discussion Topics**

Make every meeting trigger actions by ensuring each topic ends with a
"who/what/when" – *who's* doing *what* action, by *when*?

Reinforce these actions in a future-focused, follow-up email ("actions
you're doing tomorrow", not "things we discussed yesterday").

This technique could save me _____ minutes per day.

×4

This would equate to _____ hours per year.

11

When you want to run punchy, interesting and effective update meetings (or not have them)

Update meetings often swap information, but little else.

And, let's face it, they're often plain dull. They're a series of lengthy monologues, rather than value-adding discussions. They're also too long.

In fact, here's an idea: don't have one for the next two weeks. Meet again in Week Three and start with "Well, did you miss them?"

Depending on the response, either stop them entirely, or change them to only include the bits people missed. After all, meetings should be about usefulness, not habit.

Now, I recognize that stopping them might be a step too far for some teams. In fact, one of my customers once gave me this brief:

"I want us to *meet* regularly.
I want us to *update* each other.
But I don't want us to have *update meetings*."

So, I devised a new approach that reduced their 60-minute meetings down to 10, made them more interesting, generated more discussion, and always led to positive next steps.

All I did was suggest that they replace update meetings with LION meetings, where each attendee has one minute to present their LION:

Last week – How things have progressed with the activity they told you last week that they'd do this week.

Improve – Something that went well during the week.

Obstacle – A current challenge they'd like help with.

Next week – Their key deliverables for next week (in next week's LION meeting, their **L** will relay how this went).

LIONs work well because:

- Giving your team a time limit ensures they're punchy, interesting and focused (this is better than giving them a maximum number of slides, since that just encourages them to write small).
- Asking them to do an **I** and **O** means they put both sides of what's happened, rather than being only positive or negative or, more boringly, neutral – "I'm working on X".
- The **O**'s subtitle "A current challenge *they'd like help with*" ensures they come with a solution-focus, rather than just grumbling about something.
- The **L** and **N** ensures momentum and accountability: they have to look forward with their **N**s, then report back with their **L**s.

If you find templates useful, here's one to share with your team:

LION meeting on [DATE]

We want to know what you're working on. So, please bring your LION to our next meeting, where you'll have *60 seconds* to tell us:

Last week I said I'd _____ (1). What happened was _____.

Improve – something that's gone well this week is _____.

Obstacle – a challenge I'd like your help with is _____.

Next week, the main things I'm going to do are _____ (2)

Notes:
*(1) This week's **L** is an update of last week's **N**.*
*(2) Please tell us how you get on with this week's **N***
*in next week's **L**.*

And here's an example of how one might look:

LION meeting on *Monday 28th*

We want to know what you're working on. So, please bring your LION to our next meeting, where you'll have *60 seconds* to tell us:

Last week I said I'd *prepare slides for my conference keynote.* What happened was *I did them. I showed them to John and got them signed off. I'm now ready!*

Improve – Something that's gone well this week is *I finally found a supplier to manage our social media messaging.*

Obstacle – A challenge I'd like your help with is *my peer in another department appears too busy to take my calls. And I need his help, like, now.*

Next week, the main things I'm going to do are:

1. To brief in the social media campaign
2. Meet James to progress the Joint Venture discussions

One final point: if you're doing a follow-up email to your LION meeting, please don't call it "FYI". It wipes out all your good work. The next chapter explains why FYIs don't work, and what to do instead.

Build Your Snowball: Run Punchy, Interesting and Effective Update Meetings (or don't have them)

Replace update meetings with LION meetings, where each attendee has one minute to present their LION:

Last week – How things have progressed with the activity they told you last week that they'd do this week.

Improve – Something that went well during the week.

Obstacle – A current challenge they'd like help with.

Next week – Their key deliverables for next week (in next week's LION meeting, their **L** will relay how this went).

And *don't* call your follow-up email FYI!

This technique could save me _____ minutes per day.

×4

This would equate to _____ hours per year.

12

When you want to get a quick response to an FYI email

Here are five questions. You have two seconds to answer each:

QUICK QUIZ 1

1. What's the opposite of "not in"?

2. What do cows drink?

3. What weighs more – a ton of metal or a ton of feathers?

4. How much dirt is in a hole measuring 2 meters by 3 meters by 4 meters?

5. Why's the word "gullible" been removed from the dictionary?

How did you get on?

The answers are:

- In
- Water
- The same
- None
- It hasn't

Did you get them all? Or did you say:

- Out
- Milk
- Metal
- 24m^2
- "Really? I never knew that."

THE PROBLEM WITH SPEED

We make such quick decisions sometimes that we sacrifice accuracy for speed. And while we don't have to get everything 100% right, things do need to be "right enough".

When you spend the "right enough" amount of time preparing communications, you get things "right enough" first time. This saves lots of follow-up, grief and hassle.

It sounds so obvious. But, here's another quick quiz:

QUICK QUIZ 2

Do you ever...

1. Send things "FYI" without giving it any thought?

2. Turn up to chair a meeting, totally unprepared?

3. Show slides from last time's presentation, even when some aren't relevant to this time's?

4. Forget to spell-check?

5. Say "I need you to", rather than "Please can you"?

How did you get on?

By the way, the answers *should* be no, no, no, no and no

GETTING GOOD RESPONSES TO FYIs

I want to look again at Quiz 2's FYI question.

Why? Because FYIs are big communication time-wasters, for both you and the recipient. To explain this, let's look at it in a different context.

> **Scenario 1:** Mrs. X has a book she thinks Mr. Y might want to read. She runs to his desk, throws the book at him, says "Read this" and walks away.

Doesn't that seem odd behaviour? Why would Mrs. X do something like this? What's Mr. Y going to think? What's he supposed to do with the book? Why will he think she's given it to him? Will he be grateful to her? Confused by her? Will he read it?

If you didn't work in the corporate world, you'd think this second scenario was weird. But it's actually the same thing as Scenario 1. In both cases, somebody has thrown something at somebody, saying "Read this".

When you send something "FYI", what are you are expecting the recipient to do? Read it? File it? Absorb it? Act on it? Email you their views? Any of these? None? Does it matter? Will they care? Do you?

Or, as I once read, when you send an FYI, do you really mean "You're not interested in this, but I've covered my back by sending it to you".

> **Scenario 2:** Mrs. X emails Mr. Y an attachment with the message "FYI".

POWERFUL ALTERNATIVES TO FYI

The best alternatives to FYI contain:

1. A scene-set, to give context; and
2. An action, to give direction.

So, alternatives would include:

"The attached relates to X that we discussed yesterday. Have a look and tell me if you think it changes anything."
"I received this from Emma, and think it might help us with X. Check out section 3. Should we change our approach?"

"Head Office sent the attached to me, concerning X. I haven't time to read it now, but think it might interest you, because of Y. Please have a read and feedback anything you think I need to know."

These take a little longer than "FYI" – though not much, to be honest – but are much better for the reader, and therefore for you.

And, of course, when you *receive* FYIs, just reply with "Thanks for this. What would you like me to do with it?"

After all, you would *never* throw a book at someone, saying "Read this". So why do the equivalent by email?

Build Your Snowball: Get a Quick Response to an FYI Email

There are no tips in this chapter, it's just FYI...

Only joking!

The main problem with FYIs is that people don't know what to do with them. So, instead of calling it 'FYI', state:

1. A scene-set ("This relates to X").
2. An action ("Please can you do Y").

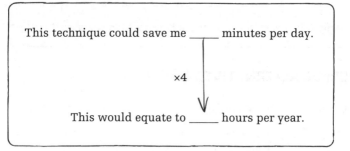

This technique could save me _____ minutes per day.

×4

This would equate to _____ hours per year.

13

When you want to empty your inbox

Cluttered inboxes are a drain on your time, your focus and your will to live.

And, as you've just seen, when quite a few of your emails are called "FYI", it's even worse.

It's imperative you learn how to unclutter them. The McKinsey study I referred to in this section's introduction found that people spend 28% of their week reading/answering emails. That's over 500 hours per year. Or, if you have a 30-year career, that's eight years of it!

The good news is, there are only three possible causes of having a full inbox, in that you have emails you've:

1.   Never opened; and/or
2.   Opened more than once – "It's not urgent. I'll deal with it later"; and/or
3.   Opened, dealt with and left there.

This means there are only three steps to emptying your inbox:

1.   Receive fewer emails.
2.   *Never* look at emails twice.
3.   Remove them when you've finished with them.

Here are simple ways to achieve all three . . .

HOW TO RECEIVE FEWER EMAILS

The best ways to do this are to:

Send fewer emails
Your inbox will contain replies to your emails. Could any of yours have been phone calls or chats instead?

I first recommended this approach to someone who'd said "I don't have time to implement your techniques. I've received 127 emails during the 90 minutes we've been in here". I asked him to look how many began with "RE", to which he counted 88. In other words, *two-thirds* had been people replying to him.

In summary: send less; you receive less.

Proactively request less emails
Where appropriate, contact people who send you emails that you don't want/need and (politely and carefully) tell them not to send them.

Do so by explaining the benefits *to them* of changing their approach: "My inbox is rammed. I'll be able to reply much more quickly if you just pick up the phone/send me a text."

HOW TO ENSURE YOU *NEVER* LOOK AT EMAILS TWICE

If you open, close and leave an email in your inbox, you are *definitely* going to look at it again.

Even more annoyingly, because you deal with important emails straight away, the ones you keep looking at are often the unimportant ones that are never important enough to deal with.

The only way to stop doing this is by never opening, closing and leaving it there. Instead, you have these choices – my five Ds:

The D	Do this when...
Deal with it	...the email requires a quick, easy or urgent response. Then file/delete the original.
Delete it	...you'll never need it again. For instance, if you've had seven round-robin "reply all" emails, delete the bottom six since the most recent contains the full chain.
Delegate it	...someone else can handle it. Then file/delete the original.
Drag it to a folder	...you want to keep it, but it needs no response. This is often worth considering for FYIs.
Diarize it	...you have to deal with it yourself, but can do so later. Transfer it into a previously set-up daily diary entry called "Answer non-urgent emails". Then, address it when your diary tells you to.

HOW TO REMOVE EMAILS ONCE YOU'VE FINISHED WITH THEM

This is now straightforward, because each **D** results in the email leaving your inbox.

Even better, each **D** only takes 30 seconds max. – often, much less. So, in the next 20 minutes, you could remove at least 40 emails.

Build Your Snowball: Empty Your Inbox

To empty your inbox:

- Receive less emails in the first place by (a) sending less and/or (b) politely asking regular senders to contact you in different ways.
- Ensure you *never* look at an email twice, by using one of the five Ds – Deal, Delete, Delegate, Drag or Diarize.
- Always remove an email from your inbox once you've looked at it.

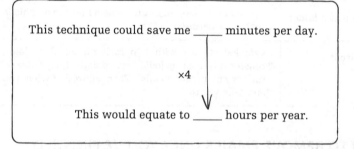

This technique could save me _____ minutes per day.

×4

This would equate to _____ hours per year.

14

When you want to see how much extra time you've now got

Let's see how much time this section will save you. Copy each chapter's time saving into this table and add them up:

Chapter – when you want to...	Minutes saved per day	Hours saved per year (*)
ensure people do what you want immediately		
find the time to communicate brilliantly		
impress senior audiences, when you haven't much time		
ensure people remember your key messages		
quickly create presentations that work		
have better, quicker meetings and conference calls		
only attend the meetings you need to		
prepare for meetings in the right way		

(Continued)

Chapter – when you want to...	Minutes saved per day	Hours saved per year (*)
ensure meetings generate actions, not just discussion topics		
run punchy, interesting and effective update meetings (or not have them)		
get a quick response to an FYI email		
empty your inbox		
Total		

(* calculated by multiplying the middle column's numbers by four)

When you add up your savings, you'll see you've a pretty big total. Remember, 50 minutes a day equals 200 hours a year. That's an entire month!

There'll never be a better opportunity to start saving this time than now, when it's fresh. And, the great thing is, because you communicate all the time, it's relatively easy to identify the first time you can try it (which, as you saw with the chapter 2 "Buy bread" example, is critical).

So, in the next few minutes, you'll be talking, emailing, writing … Which technique will you use first?

SECTION C

Persuade more people to say "yes"

How to convince others to do what you want

WHY THIS MATTERS

Your life sure would be a whole lot easier if everyone just said "yes" to you all the time.

You'd have the job of your dreams, pots of money, and you'd never feel stifled, frustrated or bored.

I guess your life's not like that?

The fact is, it can be extremely hard to get a "yes". And it's not surprising. Other people are busy. They have their own priorities and agendas, which you may not fit into. They'll have hundreds of ideas to consider, not just yours.

Given these challenges, you can see why people sometimes resort to using their authority to persuade – shouting at their children, pulling rank at work, and so on.

But, although this might get a "yes", it's often not an enthusiastic one. This reminds me of a line from the film *The Break Up*, where Jennifer Aniston's character says to Vince Vaughan, her husband "I want you to *want* to do the washing up".

Persuasion's like this. You want people to *want* to do what you ask.

Fortunately, as you're about to discover, there are many simple ways you can get much better at this.

15

When you want to understand what really motivates people

People see things so differently from us, that it can be hard to understand their thinking.

I was reminded of this the other day when I told my three-year-old I'd brush her hair. She patted my arm and said in a very patronizing voice: "No you won't. Daddies don't brush hair. When you're older, and your eyebrows are smaller, then you'll be a woman. And *then* you can brush my hair."

I'm not quite sure where she got this new view of human biology from, but I await my forthcoming female years with interest . . .

This story is an example of how people can read all sorts of weird and wonderful things into what they hear you say. It can sometimes be baffling how much they misinterpret you. It's not their fault. It's not yours either. The communication just hasn't worked.

But, to get a "yes" from them, it's important to understand what drives them. And this often isn't what you think it is. Keeping with the hair theme:

> To a wig salesman, I appear an ideal customer (one quick glance at my photo will explain why).
>
> Except I'm not.
>
> You see, hair and I don't get on. Never have. I've no interest in owning a wig.
>
> Even though I *need* one, I don't *want* one.
>
> Instead, a wig salesman's best bet is to find someone who *wants* a wig. This could well be someone who already has lots of hair.

So people's decisions are often motivated – rightly or wrongly – by what they *want*, not what they *need*.

This means that trying to persuade by explaining that someone *needs* something often doesn't work. It's better to show your idea helps them get more of what they *want*:

- "You *need* to send me your update" is not as effective as "Let's get this project off your desk as soon as possible. To help me do this, please could you send me your update".
- "You *need* to attend that meeting" is not as persuasive as "I want to make it easier for you to make quicker decisions. To help with this, there's a meeting next week which . . ."
- Instead of "You *need* to reply to my proposal", try "To make sure you achieve your objectives as quickly as possible, please can I ask you to hit reply and . . ."

Communicating like this can sometimes feel weird, especially if you're convinced they do *need* it. But, communication's all about the audience, not you. And when people email me saying they "need me" to do something, I'm always tempted to reply (but am yet to do so) with "Well, *I need you* to learn some manners".

This chapter's useful in that it helps explain what motivates people. The next chapter builds on this, by showing what to *say*, so you actually *do* motivate them.

Build Your Snowball: Understand What Really Motivates People

To get more, quicker "yeses", engage people by focusing on what they *want*, not *need*.

16

When you want to say things that excite people

People are more likely to say "yes" when they see it's in their interest to do so. This means it's important to:

1. Know what's important to them; and
2. Align your proposal to this.

This sounds obvious; but most people don't do this well. Or consistently. Or *ever*. If they were better at it, you wouldn't hear such phrases as:

- Why should I do that?
- It's too expensive.
- This meeting is tedious. Why am I here?
- I haven't time to respond to this.
- I know what you want me to do, but it's not a priority to me right now.

BE BENEFITS-BASED, NOT FEATURES-FOCUSED

To engage people, focus on what *benefits* them. The best way to define what I mean by a "benefit" is to contrast it with its opposite, a "feature".

A "feature" *describes* something. A "benefit" explains how someone's *future is enhanced* by it:

- "This toothpaste is minty" = feature: it describes the toothpaste.
- "This toothpaste will help your breath smell nice" = benefit: it shows why you'll be better off after using it.

So, you buy because of the benefits (your beautiful breath), not the features (the mintiness).

Similarly, if someone's résumé said "I've worked in many different sectors. Do you want me?", you'd say "no". That's a feature of them; you care about the *benefit to you* of them working in different sectors.

Or when a meeting's agenda said "We'll be discussing X. Do you want to come?", you'd say "no" unless you happened to care passionately about X (and how often does *that* happen?!)

Sometimes, people try to make things sound beneficial, by using wonderful adjectives. But "This toothpaste is the mintiest on the planet" is still not a benefit. It's *describing* how uniquely wonderful the toothpaste is. And, because it's *describing*, it's a feature – albeit a unique, glorious one.

I'm not saying features are irrelevant. In fact, if some are missing – like, for example, "suitable experience" – you won't be considered a viable alternative in the first place. But these features are like a gambler's table stakes: they let you play the game, but they don't mean you'll *win* the game.

Here are three simple rules about what makes a good benefit:

1. They focus on the other person, so usually contain the word "you".
2. It's only a benefit if the other person – *not you* – perceives it as such.
3. Benefits happen in the future, because they haven't happened yet. This future-focus led me to suggest the word "AFTERs" instead of "benefits". In other words, why are they better off AFTER communicating with you? I've found the word "AFTERs" helps people focus on improving the other person's *future* (see chapter 1 for more on AFTERs).

These three elements help you see whether you're saying things others will find in their interest. For instance:

When you say...	Rule 1: "You"	Rule 2: Perceived by them	Rule 3: Future	Reason
"FYI."	✗	✗	✗	Nobody cares.
"Read this – it'll ensure you're ready for Wednesday's board meeting."	✓	✓	✓	This would grab someone's attention.
"Founded in 1922."	✗	✗	✗	Almost nobody cares.
"This will reduce your tax bill" (said to an adult).	✓	✓	✓	A good benefit to a tax payer.
"This will reduce your tax bill" (said to a young child).	✓	✗	✓	Irrelevant to a child.

There are many benefits *to you* of knowing what the other person perceives to be a benefit. The next two chapters cover two of the best ones:

- How to align your agenda with theirs.
- How to persuade them to say "yes" more easily.

Build Your Snowball: Say Things That Excite People

To sell your ideas, your propositions or yourself: explain how much you'll benefit the other person, remembering that benefits have three elements:

1. They contain the word "you".
2. The other person (not you) perceives it's a benefit.
3. It relates to their future.

Emphasize these benefits throughout, especially at the start – this engages people early.

17

When you want to align your agenda to everyone else's

Have you ever been bored during someone else's communication?

Has anyone ever been bored during yours?

It's notoriously hard to align your agenda with someone else's. But failing to do so causes big problems – people don't buy-in, strategies don't land, stakeholders don't engage, teams don't function, families argue . . . the list is endless.

In short, if you don't adapt your messages, people aren't persuaded. Communications take too long. They don't work.

IDENTIFY "WHY THAT'S GOOD"

To help align agendas, prepare your communications by playing the "Why's That Good Game", where you imagine:

- Your audience saying *"Why's that good?"* to your agenda; and
- You replying with *"Well, it's good for you because"*.

So, for a leader outlining her new strategy:

Leader: Here's the new strategy.
Team: Why's that good?
Leader: Well, it's good for you because you'll know the direction we're going.
Team: Why's that good?
Leader: Well, it's good for you because you'll know how your role is changing.
Team: Why's that good?

> Leader: Well, it's good for you because you'll learn some simple changes to make, to help you be more successful and to enjoy your job more.

See how it works? The bottom line (about success and enjoyment) is much more compelling than the first (the strategy).

This example's very *positive*. I used "why's that *good*" to show what someone could *gain*.

Instead, you can go the other way. After all, "fear of loss" is often the strongest motivator. So, you could be *negative*, using "why's that *bad* if I *don't* hear this?":

> Leader: Here's the new strategy.
> *Team: Why's that bad if I don't hear this?*
> Leader: Well, it's bad for you because you won't know what's going on.
> *Team: Why's that bad?*
> Leader: Well, it's bad for you because you'll make the wrong decisions.
> *Team: Why's that bad?*
> Leader: Well, it's bad for you because you'll get left behind the rest of us.

SAY THE "BEST BIT" FIRST

In both examples, the last sentence is the most persuasive. So, to trigger instant buy-in, start at the end and work backwards, saying your agenda (in this case, "the strategy") last. For instance, with the first example:

> *"I want to show you simple changes to make, to help you be more successful, and to enjoy your job more. To help you do this, I'm going to show you how your role is changing, by outlining the direction we're going. I'll do this by sharing our new strategy with you."*

And using the second:

> *"I want to make sure you don't get left behind the rest of us because of making the wrong decisions. This might happen if you don't know what's going on this coming year. So, I'm going to give you all the info you need, by running through our new strategy."*

So, the same topic (new strategy) can lead to two benefits – a positive-increaser (success/enjoyment) and a negative-reducer (not getting left behind). You would use the most compelling and appropriate one to introduce your topic.

A word of warning about negatives: they're powerful and – as the saying goes – "with great power comes great responsibility". Sending an email called "This will stop you getting fired" won't help your Employee Engagement scores much.

The message here is simple but powerful: start your communications with *their* agenda, and *they're* more likely to buy into yours.

The next chapter builds on this, by showing how to ensure they do.

Build Your Snowball: Align Your Agenda to Everyone Else's

To help people see how your messages relate to them, play the "Why's That Good Game":

- Start with your agenda.
- Imagine them saying *"Why's that good?"*
- To which you keep replying *"Well, it's good for you because"* until it becomes their agenda.
- If appropriate, repeat the exercise, but with "why it's *bad* if you *don't*".
- Choose the more powerful benefit and start your communication with that. This helps you engage them *instantly*.

18

When you want to get an enthusiastic "yes" very quickly

When someone wants you to agree to something, you're more likely to when:

- You know that saying "yes" will benefit you; and
- "No" doesn't seem to be an option.

Unfortunately, people often omit one or both of these, which is why they hear "no" so frequently. To show what I mean, imagine you were one of the following three people.

Situation 1: The direct report

You're extremely busy, working on an important document with a tight deadline. One of your direct reports interrupts you, asking "Have you got five minutes?"

There are only two responses you can give: "No, not now", or "Yes, but please be quick".

Not what they wanted.

Situation 2: The salesperson

You're buying new IT. The salesperson says "Here's our proposed IT system covering everything we discussed. It will cost you £100,000. Would you like to buy it?"

You *might* say "Yes please", but you're more likely to give one of two responses: "Maybe, but not exactly as you're proposing" or "Maybe, but could you do anything about the price?"

Again, not what they wanted.

Situation 3: The child

You're a soccer-obsessed, 12-year-old boy. Your father says "Do you want to go to bed tonight at 8pm?"

This time there's only one answer: "No".

BO: A BETTER WAY TO GET A "YES"

Can you see why these three situations didn't work? In each:

- It wasn't in your interest to say "yes". There were *no* reasons why you should agree (in fact, there were many why you shouldn't); and
- Each request was a yes/no question, meaning you could reply "no". So you did.

So, what should people do instead? Well, one effective technique is to use **BO**, which stands for:

B – Benefits: explain why it's in their interest to say "Yes". These must be the benefits from *their* perspective, not yours, so they see they're better off agreeing with you.

O – Options: give them 2–3 choices as to how they accept. This gives them a yes/yes choice, rather than a yes/no. In other words, don't ask *if* they want it; ask *which* they want.

Now let's apply BO to three situations, but this time imagining it's *you* who's asking.

Situation 1: The direct report

Want five minutes with your boss? Try:

> *"I'm keen to finish that report you asked for, but could do with five minutes with you to discuss a couple of points in the Executive Summary. Have you got the time now, or would you prefer later today?"*

This turns the boss's thinking from "Do I give him five minutes?" to *"When* do I give him five minutes?"

Situation 2: The salesperson

Looking to sell an IT solution? Go with:

> *"We've agreed this IT will help your business be more efficient. There are a few ways we could progress this. You'll get best results if we do everything we've discussed today. This will cost £100,000. But I know money is tight. So, a cheaper option would be to remove standalone phases 3 and 6, which would reduce the price to £65,000. Which do you think will be most appropriate?"*

This changes "Do I buy?" to *"Which* do I buy?"

Situation 3: The child

And now imagine you have a soccer-loving son. This is easy for me – I do. You'll get much more joy with:

> *"Jack, let's play soccer tomorrow before everyone else is up. Obviously this means we'll need a good night's rest before the Big Game. So, when do you want to go to bed – 7.30pm or 8pm?"*

This works every time. Believe me, I know: I use BO to get Jack to go to bed every day!

In fact, BO works extraordinarily well in pretty much every situation. It's great for conversations, quick requests and as your final line when you're seeking agreement. But, it's "only" a persuasive couple of sentences. And before you say your BO, you first have to prove you can bring the other person the value they want. The next chapter shows how to do this.

Build Your Snowball: Get an Enthusiastic "Yes" Very Quickly

To secure willing agreement, use **BO** (Benefit–Options). This approach gives the other person:

• A reason to say "yes".
• A choice as to how they do so.

If either's missing, it's less likely to work.

19

When you want to prove you're someone's best option

There are famous stories of expensive missed opportunities:

- Many record companies turned down the Beatles; like Decca, who said "The Beatles have no future in show business".
- Twelve publishers rejected J.K. Rowling's 200-page script for Harry Potter.
- Disney once sacked John Lasseter – he's now their Chief Creative Officer.

But you don't hear too many of these stories. Why? Because the only time you do is when the "no" goes on to become a spectacular success elsewhere.

So, people often find it safer to say "no" than "yes". After all, which is more likely to be flagged as a mistake?

- Agreeing to something that fails, and makes you rue the day you said "yes"? Or,
- Rejecting an opportunity that therefore never happens, so nobody can say whether it was a bad idea to turn it down?

When you look at it like that, you can see why people often say "no". They think it just does less harm. And this makes it very hard to persuade certain people to say "yes" to you.

So, you have to *prove* they'll benefit by agreeing. After all, it's easier to persuade people when they view *you* as an expert in an area *they* aren't. This helps them know their best option is to do what you advise. In effect, they let you make the decision for them. Here are a few ways to do this.

Proof point	It works because...	How to make it more powerful
Case study	Shows you've succeeded with similar things before.	Don't say things in the usual chronological "case study order" – background, your work, their results. That puts the best bit at the end, when people are less attentive. Instead, start with the results: "I can help you deliver your cost reduction targets. I helped my previous company reduce costs by £3 million, by doing..."
Testimonials	Gives credible third-party evidence you can deliver.	Choose someone whose name will impress. Ensure their comment focuses on the impact you *caused*, rather than the work you *did*. So, "After John got involved, we reduced our costs by £3 million ", Mrs. X, CFO, Y Ltd. Ask the author's permission to use it.
Reference	Let's them speak to someone who's experienced your work.	This works well when they know and/or are impressed by your referee. Again, ask the referee's permission first.
Your process	Explains what you'll be doing, and why it's better than the alternatives.	Use a title that incorporates the main benefit you're bringing. So, replace "Our process" with "How we can save £3 million ". Differentiate it from: the alternatives, by being clear about your "cxtras" (see the Plumber Slides in Chapter 39). the "doing nothing" option, by showing the downside of continuing as they are (see Walloping in Chapter 4).

(Continued)

Proof point	It works because...	How to make it more powerful
Free advice	Makes them think "I'd not thought of that. What else does she know that I don't?"	Include your new ideas, techniques, statistics, top tips, advice about likely problems, credible research... *anything* that takes their thinking to a new place.
Lists of people/ companies you've helped	Shows you know what you're doing (and people often follow the crowd).	Ensure the names you choose are: their peers; and/or jaw-dropping, so they think "wow, so you work with *them!*"
Your credentials	Shows you're qualified to do it.	Ensure you say things others can't. Two companies recently pitched to me and separately said they had "market leading advice". Well, they both couldn't have done!
Financials that stack up	Proves the numbers work.	Make sure your numbers are accurate (get them checked?) and easy to understand.
Different pricing options	Lets them choose their risk level.	Offer different options for them to choose between (standard or deluxe) and/or a conditional price structure – "if X happens, you pay £Y".
Awards	Shows you're better than your peers.	Use recent awards, in relevant fields, given for your achievement with similar companies/areas.
PR	Suggests you "must be good" if people are writing about you.	As with awards, use recent PR, relating to relevant achievements.

This table isn't an exhaustive list – no doubt you can think of others – but contains the type of thing you should be looking for. Remember:

- No proofs – likely to get a "no".
- Generic, bland proofs – still "no".
- Some of the table's proofs – a "yes" is much more likely.

How many proofs do you need? Well, as you'll see in the next chapter "When you want to make a sale", it's less than people think. Think quality not quantity. The aim is as few as possible. So, start with your most persuasive. If that works, you only needed one. If not, go to the second, then third.

Build Your Snowball: Prove You're Someone's Best Option

To persuade someone to choose you, use some of: case studies, testimonials, references, your process, free advice, lists of previous beneficiaries of your input, your credentials, financials, different pricing options, awards, and/or PR.

Use this chapter's table to make sure they're more impactful than everyone else's.

20

When you want to make a sale

If you work in sales, I imagine:

1. You have stretching targets.
2. You're short of time.

So I wanted to create a short chapter to address both of these, by explaining my five steps to winning a sale. To keep this chapter as punchy as possible:

- Some of the steps are expanded on elsewhere in the book. If you want to read more, I've added the chapter references for you; and
- The next chapter shows how to incorporate these steps into your proposals and sales presentations.

Before running through the steps, here are my three Golden Rules of Sales:

> **Rule #1: The customer is the most important person, so give her the information she needs to make the best decision.**

> **Rule #2: The customer will buy when she knows you're the one best placed to improve her future.**

> **Rule #3: When the customer says "Yes", shut up.**

These rules mean we no longer use some traditional sales messages. After all, when you say:

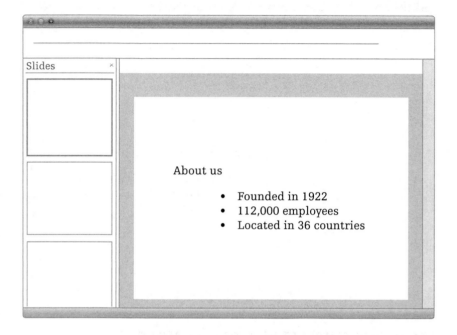

Customers see:

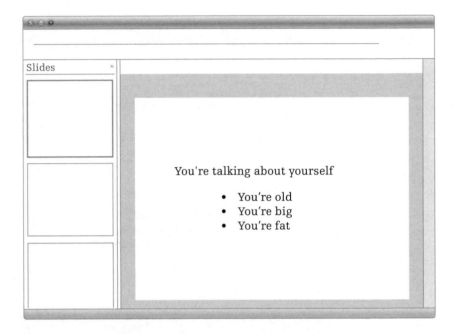

ABCDE: THE SIMPLEST WAY TO SELL MORE

My five steps of selling are:

AFTERs – Find the customer's desired future

Be certain – State you can help them

Convince – Prove you can help them

Deal with objections – Remove their concerns

Electives – Offer options that they can choose between

Looking at each in turn:

AFTERs – Find the customer's desired future

Since selling is all about helping the customer achieve their desired *future* (Rule #2), start by finding what this *future* is. In other words, why they'll be better off AFTER working with you. (Chapter 31 has much more detail on AFTERs.)

The two best ways to uncover their AFTERs are by *asking* and *guiding* them:

Asking means using Future-Based Questions (FBQs) to uncover their desired AFTERs, like:

- What are you looking to achieve?
- What are your goals/objectives?
- How will you know our work has been a success?

FBQs work well, as long as the customer knows the answers. Sometimes, a better approach is:

Guiding, where you help shape their thinking, either by:

- Splitting their future into manageable bits, to help them focus. For example, I could say to a sales director: "There are three elements to 'selling': having the right mindset; seeing the right buyers; and saying the right words when in front of them. Which of these do your people need most guidance with?" Or,
- Using your research/insights to open their eyes to new possibilities: "The Sales Executive Council found that 91% of buyers don't think value-to-price is the biggest driver of customer loyalty. This means your current focus on reducing price probably isn't the best approach. Let's discuss a couple of alternatives to see what we can help you achieve."

Once you've uncovered the AFTERs:

- Repeat them back to the customer, ensuring they agree; and
- Ask the customer to prioritize them. This tells you their #1 AFTER, which is very important information for the rest of the sale. See the next chapter on proposals/presentations for more on this.

Worked example – step 1

Let's assume that you uncover they only have one AFTER: to successfully export into Belgium.

Be certain – State you can help them

Customers want to feel *certain* you can help them. So when you're *certain* you can deliver their AFTERs, say so: "We can *definitely help you* with that" or "I'm *completely confident* we can help you achieve those objectives."

Whereas the **A** of **ABCDE** – uncovering AFTERs – takes a while, step **B** takes 10 seconds max. It's just one sentence. But it's important: it starts to build their feelings of certainty.

> **Worked example – step 2**
>
> "We can *definitely help you* export into Belgium."

Convince – Prove you can help them

If you're very lucky, when you say step **B**'s "We can definitely help you", the customer will say "Great. Let's start". If this happens, remember Golden Rule #3 – the customer's said "Yes", so shut up! Get the order book out and crack on.

In all my life, this has only happened to me once. (It was great when it did!) But in practice your next step will be to convince them that you *can* definitely help them.

There are lots of ways to do this – chapter 19 discussed lots of them. In our example though, some could be:

> **Worked example – step 3**
>
> - The case study of company X who you helped expand into Belgium.
> - A testimonial: "Your Company helped us build our market share in Belgium from 0% to 12% in two years". Mrs. X, job title Y, company Z.
> - A list of all the customers you've helped with Belgium and/or exports.
> - Your process for entering Belgium, and why it's different/better than everybody else's.
> - Free advice about Belgium, to show you know things that they don't.

Deal with objections – Remove their concerns

Customers will probably have some concerns about buying from you – your price, your experience, your impressive competition, they might feel it's easier to do nothing, and so on.

You *must* address these. If you don't, they might never get dealt with. This means they won't buy.

There are two ways to uncover, and then remove, their concerns:

- Ask them what they are: "So, we know that we can help. But it's what *you* think that counts! What are your concerns about us working together on this project?"
- Use your experience/common sense to guess, and weave these into your sales discussion: "If I was you, I might be worried about X. Is that the case?" or "Some of our best customers were originally concerned about X. Are you?"

Then, of course, you have to persuasively remove these concerns (chapter 53 has loads of techniques for doing this). After all, if someone said they were worried about cost, you wouldn't follow that with "Yes, you're right. It is a lot"!

Work example – step 4

"If I was you, I might be concerned that we haven't worked together before, and that giving such an important campaign to a new partner is risky. Is that the case?"

[Yes, it does feel uncomfortable]

"Well, I totally understand that. In fact, a couple of our best customers originally thought the same thing. Do you mind if I explain how we can overcome this?"

Electives – Offer options that they can choose between

When you give someone a "Yes/No" choice ("Our proposal will cost you £120,000 – do you want it or not?"), you can't complain if they choose "No".

So, offer the customer 2–3 different options, and work with them to choose the one they feel is best for them. Use chapter 18's BO approach to do this.

Also, before giving the price, remind them of the value, so the price then looks the excellent value for money that it is.

Worked example – step 5

So, we've agreed your projected returns from our work will be £1–2 million in the first year. There are a couple of ways we can help you achieve this: we could do X for £50,000 or Y for a total of £75,000. Which option do you prefer?

By now, you might be thinking ABCDE sounds obvious. After all, all I'm saying is that you find what the customer wants to achieve, prove you can help them get there, and ask how they want to proceed.

However, knowing the steps and doing them *every time* are two very different things. This quick self-test might help. How does your company stack up?

Self-test

1. How often do you know a customer's desired AFTERs?
   Every sale
   Most sales
   If there's time to find out
   Never
2. How many times have you gone for a sale which, in retrospect, you shouldn't have? On these occasions, if you'd asked better questions, might you have pulled out sooner?
3. How often do you state *with certainty* that you can give the customer what they want? Do you say it as early as possible in the process?
4. When proving you can do the job:
   How often do you talk about your process (not persuasive) compared to giving third-party evidence that you can deliver results (very persuasive)?
   If you use third-party evidence, how often do you mention it early in your sales communications? (I've seen them first appear on page 50 of an 80-page proposal. They should be prominently placed early, including in Executive Summaries).
   Are your most persuasive proofs easy to spot, or are they hidden in the middle of sections/paragraphs/slides?
5. Does every salesperson in your company always work hard to uncover the customer's objections? Do you have a standard approach for removing them?
6. Do you always offer options?
7. Does your marketing material (website, brochures and so on) follow this approach? Or do they focus more on describing your company and services?

Unless you scored 100%, you can be even more AFTERs-y than you are now. And doing so makes a huge difference to even the best people. For instance, one of my customers – Marc Berendes – was very successful before I met him:

- He'd reached the top of commercial finance within a global division at a young age.
- He'd then changed career to become general manager of the fourth largest affiliate worldwide, aged just 40.
- His three children – all still at primary school – each speaks four languages.

So, a successful guy! But he found AFTERs-based selling took him up another level: "AFTERs completely changed the way we presented offers to customers. After taking my new job and witnessing the ineffectiveness of our offer presentation, we changed everything, so it became based on the customer and their AFTERs. This has helped us to win many more deals."

The great thing about selling is you can always improve. Which one thing can you take from this chapter to help you be more successful?

 Build Your Snowball: Make a Sale

When selling, remember the three Golden Rules:

Rule #1: the customer is the most important person, so give her the information she needs to make the best decision.

Rule #2: the customer will buy when she *knows* you are the one best placed to improve her *future*.

Rule #3: when the customer says "Yes", shut up.

And the five steps of convincing a customer to buy:

AFTERs – Find their desired future.
Be certain – State you can help them achieve it.
Convince – Prove you can help them achieve it.
Deal with objections – Remove their concerns.
Electives – Offer options that they can choose between.

21

When you want to write a winning proposal or sales presentation

Some of the most boring communications I've ever seen have been proposals and sales presentations – overlong, too detailed, minimal focus on the customer, similar to the competition's, and similar to proposals the sales team sent to a different customer last week.

It would be a real shame if any communication was this ineffective. But, with something that's supposed to convince a customer to choose you ahead of the competition? Well, that's more than a shame.

This chapter shows how to bring your content together in a persuasive, compelling structure so the customer knows you can help them. You'll notice that this structure follows ABCDE described in the previous chapter.

I've split it into the two common situations where you:

- Are starting a sales communication from scratch; and
- Have a first draft in your hand, and need to improve it quickly.

But, before that, here are three important guidelines with proposals.

1. Don't write proposals too early

It's usually easier to convince someone verbally than in writing.

So keep talking with the customer until you've both agreed a way you could work together. And only *then* send a proposal which confirms your discussions.

The alternative – less discussion and an earlier proposal – means the document has to do most of the convincing. This isn't as likely to work. By definition, the proposal will be longer and probably contain irrelevant content.

2. Ask the customer about content

The easiest way to persuade a customer is by giving them the information they need to make a decision in your favor.

And the easiest way to discover what this information is? *Ask* them ("What information do you want to see? Would you like it detailed or in overview?" And so on).

3. Agree follow-up times in advance

Recognize this?

You send a proposal. The customer says they'll get back to you. They don't. Do you chase (and feel like you're pestering) or wait (and feel like you're powerless, and that you've been forgotten).

It's far easier to agree *before* you send the proposal when you'll speak *after* it: "I'll create a proposal based on what we've agreed and send it over tomorrow. When would you suggest we discuss it?"

CREATING SALES COMMUNICATIONS FROM SCRATCH

Sales communications often start with "About us" and end with "How we can help you". In other words, we talk about us first, and the customer second. This doesn't work:

- It's boring.
- The most interesting thing comes at the end, when they've probably switched off.
- Your competition probably did exactly the same thing.
- The customer perceives that you think you're more important than they are.

The following table shows how to structure your sales communications – both proposals and presentations – in a better way. By way of example, I've assumed that the customer has three AFTERs which, in order of priority, are to:

1. Increase exports into Belgium.
2. Enhance staff engagement.
3. Remove the needless inefficiencies that are wasting people's time.

Why not print off one of your recent sales communications, compare it with this table, and see how it stacks up?

Section	Traditional wording	Improved wording	Rationale	ABCDE?
Title	"Your proposal", or "Our proposal to X Limited."	"Helping you increase exports to Belgium."	A catchy title, which includes the customer's #1 AFTER, hooks them in early. Also, your front page/slide should be professionally designed. If they don't think "Wow" now, they probably won't for a long time.	A (#1 priority only).
Executive Summary	Thank you for asking us to propose for this contract. We are very excited to submit this proposal to you. We are experts at designing bespoke solutions in this area. We are also passionately focused on customer service. We believe this sets us apart from the competition...	We've agreed that your three main objectives from this work are to successfully: 1. Export into Belgium. 2. Enhance staff engagement. 3. Remove the time you all waste through needless inefficiencies. We can help you achieve all three. This document explains how we propose to do so, the key elements being...	Your Executive Summary should be just that: a *summary* that time-poor *executives* can read quickly. We want it to leave them thinking "This lot can *definitely* take us where we want to go."	A-C: include a very brief summary of your approach for all three AFTERs. D: remove key 1–2 objections, if it's important to do so here. E: summarize the options you're suggesting.

Section	Traditional wording	Improved wording	Rationale	ABCDE?
Contents page	Our approach. Our technical experience. Our innovation.	How we will help you access Belgium quickly. Sub-heading Sub-heading Our four steps to enhancing your staff engagement. Sub-heading Sub-heading How we'll remove your time absorbers. Sub-heading Sub-heading	You want to structure your communication around their AFTERs, not your deliverables. The only exception to this: when the customer stipulates the contents, use that.	**A** (all three AFTERs), plus relevant sub-headings.
AFTER #1 chapter	**Our approach** We have unrivalled expertise in Belgium. We have the largest network of agents, and have been working with the majority of them for over eight years. Our approach is to introduce them to you and...	**How we will access Belgium quickly** You need to access Belgium as quickly as possible. The quicker you achieve this, the quicker you surge ahead of your competition – one of your key goals. We will help you do this by...	Include all the detail about how you will deliver AFTER #1, phrased from the customer's viewpoint.	**ABCD** (for Belgium only).
AFTER #2 chapter	As above, but for AFTER #2, not #1.			**ABCD** (for staff engagement only).
AFTER #3 chapter	As above, but for AFTER #3, not #2.			**ABCD** (for time absorbers only).

(Continued)

Section	Traditional wording	Improved wording	Rationale	ABCDE?
Our options	So, we propose that we deliver X, Y and Z. The cost for this is £X. (In effect "This is it. Do you want it or not?").	We have identified three approaches we can take, to help you achieve your objectives: **Option 1: X** This option has the advantages of . . . **Option 2: X+Y** In addition, we could also . . . **Option 3: X+Y+Z** In addition, we could also . . . (In effect, "Here's a choice. Which do you prefer?")	This gives customers 2–3 choices (with associated prices), so they can pick their preference.	E
Appendix	Many proposals/ presentations don't contain appendices. But this means all the detail is in your document, which slows the reader down. This makes it harder for them to identify your main points quickly.	Include the detail the customer wants (note: not "everything you can think of") in the appendix, clearly referenced to the relevant pages.	Where appropriate, insert supporting detail in appendices, to prove that you can deliver, and/or that they don't need to worry about their objections.	CD (the detail).

This table is very useful to help prepare a proposal from scratch. But here's what to do when you've been asked to improve something that's already written . . .

EDITING FIRST DRAFTS QUICKLY

Recognize any of these?

- Someone sends you their slides at 10pm the night before your presentation.
- A colleague supplies the information you requested in the wrong format, a couple of days *after* the deadline you gave them.

It's no wonder we often have to edit sales communications so quickly!

To do this, review them through the customer's eyes (see the left-hand column below), and make the necessary adjustments (in the right):

The customer's perspective	Simple steps to improve things
Is the first impression impressive?	
Is the title good?	Play the "Why's That Good Game" with the main title (see chapter 17).
Does the communication look dauntingly long?	Shorten it, by thinking "Keep, bin, appendix" (see chapter 59).
Does the front page look like they care about me?	Professionally design the front page/slide.
Following a quick flick-through, does this seem focused on me, the customer?	
Are the titles interesting?	Play the "Why's That Good Game" with *all* titles and subtitles (see Chapter 25 about impactful titles).
Have they understood my requirements?	Make sure your introductions are persuasive, interesting and tailored (see the 4Ws in chapter 26).
Does the Executive Summary impress me?	Make sure that it comprises at least **ABC** and, when appropriate, **DE** as well.

(Continued)

The customer's perspective	Simple steps to improve things
Did my flick-through suggest that the communication would be...	
Interesting?	Ensure the pages don't all look the same. If there's a run of, say, five identical-looking pages, change the middle one (e.g. insert a visual) to break it up.
Easy to read?	Shorten paragraphs: aim for none over four lines long. Ensure there's at least one sub-heading on each page. With slides, remove as many words as possible, so they don't think you'll be reading them out.

 Build Your Snowball: Write a Winning Proposal or Sales Presentation

Remember your aim is to ensure the customer is *certain* you're best placed to deliver the AFTERs they want. Basing your structure around ABCDE, gives you the best chance of achieving this.

22

When you want to stand out from the crowd

The previous two chapters looked at how to make more sales, including how to improve your sales communications.

Another key component of selling anything – yourself, your ideas, your proposals – is that you stand out from the crowd.

After all, to convince someone to choose you, you must appear different to their alternatives. If you're not, you won't "win".

Here are six approaches to help you do this really well. One of my customers christened these the Super Six.

Method #1: Provide "wow" moments

People want amazing experiences that they remember for years. So, go the extra mile to provide them with "wow" moments.

I use the phrase "extra mile" deliberately. Most people think they do this. They don't, or it wouldn't be called "extra". It'd be "the mile that everyone always goes".

So, go extra miles to give an extra wow:

- To your customers – deliver jaw-dropping service and provide amazing add-ons they weren't expecting.
- To your colleagues – get to know them as people, fuel their passion, publicly recognize them, make your meetings/presentations exciting.

- To your boss – work hard to make yourself a pleasure to be with, provide value and insights nobody else does, make them look good, volunteer for things, come in early, stay late.

Method #2: Teach them something

If you can get someone to think "Well, I'd *never* thought of it like that", it's a great start. It ticks both boxes of you being (a) different and (b) value-adding. Nobody else has made them think this, or it wouldn't have been new to them.

For example, a couple of years ago I was asked to visit a large retail organization, to help improve their employee engagement. Before I went, I asked around, and found someone who used to work there. I asked her what she thought of the engagement and the reasons for it. She told me, then introduced me to some of her ex-colleagues, who were also very honest. These conversations led me to uncover that:

- The bosses didn't communicate with their people.
- This meant there wasn't enough information flowing around the organization.
- This led to people thinking "information is power".
- Which caused them *not* to share information they heard.
- This meant all the usual flows of information – vertical through the hierarchy, horizontal across departments – just wasn't happening.
- All of which was the main cause of low employee engagement.

When I met the Exec for the first time, I was able to share what I'd found out, and asked if they thought this was a fair reflection of the way things were. It turned out it was. And it also turned out they hadn't thought of it like that, and were delighted I'd told them. Nobody else had done.

Method #3: Facts tell, stories sell

Relaying a story about something you've achieved, and the impact it had, differentiates you. After all, nobody else can say they've done it, because you're the only one who did.

Most importantly, ensure you link your story to the needs of the person you're seeking to impress. This helps them perceive you as uniquely placed to help them, rather than you simply discussing your own genius.

For example: "You mentioned at last week's conference that you want us to be more customer-focused. I'd like to volunteer to help with this. I was part of a team that ran a similar project at my previous company, which led to market share increasing by X% in only Y months."

Also, when choosing your best stories, remember that people often want to see you can have a long-term impact (the next chapter shows how to do this), so focus more on these examples than your short-term successes.

Method #4: Use unique contacts
If you know someone who knows the person you want to impress, ask:

- Their advice on how to approach them.
- Their permission to mention their name in your meeting.
- How they want you to mention them. For example, do they want you just to say their name, or describe something they've done? Doing this ensures your interaction benefits all three of you, and almost always leads to quicker rapport-building in your meeting.

Method #5: Find a unique connection
Finding common ground accelerates the rapport-build. And it will set you apart if you're the only one who made the connection. But, beware:

- Ensure it's a real connection, not one you've assumed to be true.
- Make sure you ask them about their thoughts on your shared interest. Don't use common ground as an excuse for you to give your opinions only.
- Forced, shallow connections don't work. Once, a door-to-door salesman saw my daughter's bike outside our house. Then, when I opened the door, he blurted out "I've got children too", which was a little perturbing.

The last point is important. A lot of us are told to build rapport, but don't be too "friendly" too soon. Tony Birch – a proposal expert at Shipley Ltd. (if you write proposals, look them up: a great company) – told me of a procurement director who hated salespeople's phony rapport-building so much that he put a photograph of some children on his desk. Then, every time a salesperson spotted the photograph and said "Are they your children?", he replied "No. What do you want?"

Method #6: If you do have something unique, mention it
The last of the Super Six is to mention something unique, if you have it. This can be very powerful, but ensure that:

- Your unique thing relates to their agenda, or is fascinating enough on its own so that they want to hear more.
- It *is* unique: "I've led big teams before" isn't. Neither is "We have exceptional customer service". Everyone says this.
- You stop discussing it if they don't seem interested.

Also, be careful when discussing your unique thing. People might not be impressed by it. For instance, a taxi driver once told me he stayed in a bed and breakfast in Blackpool which had a unique thing: *no cold water*. When he asked what to do if he wanted some, the owner replied "Just run a bowl of hot water, and wait for a bit". That made that B&B *unique*, but certainly not of benefit to . . . well, anyone.

WHICH OF THE SUPER SIX IS BEST?

It depends. But use *at least* one. If you don't, you look the same as everyone else, and you're soon going to hear "So, why are you better than my alternatives?" or, more depressingly, "Can you do anything about the price?"

 Build Your Snowball: Stand Out from the Crowd

To differentiate yourself from everybody else out there, use one or more of the Super Six:

1. Provide "wow" moments – go the extra mile ("extra" as in others don't do it).
2. Teach people something – when you make them think "Well, I'd *never* thought of it like that", they see you as someone who provides unique value.
3. Facts tell, stories sell – tell relevant stories about what you've achieved and what you've helped *others* achieve. Nobody else can use your stories.
4. Use unique contacts – ask your network for advice, support and – where appropriate – name-dropping.
5. Find a unique connection – a great way to build rapport: find something you both share that most (all?) others don't.
6. If you do have something unique, mention it – but don't say something's unique if it isn't.

23

When you want to cause long-term change, not a short-term blip

People fund long-term assets (like a car) with long-term finance (a loan); and short-term assets (iPod) with short-term finance (credit card).

After all, I have yet to see someone pay for a shirt by taking out a mortgage.

Similarly if you want to persuade people to change the way they think, feel and act *forever*, you're going to have to tell them many times, over a long period of time.

We all *know* repetition works. It's why we're so good at remembering to clean our teeth and wash behind our ears: because, as children, we were reminded every day for years until it became second nature.

Given this, it's strange how people often think that one communication, given once, is going to cause long-term change:

- One-off roadshows that explain the company's new vision (this doesn't cause employees to change their mindset and priorities forever).
- Cascades with minimal follow-up (this causes messages to become diluted/lost).
- One-day workshops (these often change behaviours for a short period, before people revert back).
- Sending one email called "FYI" (this causes . . . well, nothing).

These one-offs will *never* be enough. So, what should be done instead?

Well, learn from good examples of repetition that you see around you. For example:

> When it became illegal in the UK to smoke in public places, there were adverts, media campaigns, notices everywhere – pubs, clubs, hotels, public buildings.
>
> This meant everyone heard the message many, many times. They knew it was 100% definitely happening, and wasn't a "flavor of the month" they could ignore.
>
> And then, immediately after the ban started, there were a few tabloid articles about people saying "I'm not changing. I've smoked for forty years" and the like. But, the campaign kept going. In the end, the die-hards changed. And this new law has been a huge success. It's "the way things are" now.

I guess there's a lot your company could learn from this example? Like, the unrelenting follow-up, the choice of the right media (more on this in the next chapter), and staying on course until the stragglers catch up.

SIMPLE WAYS TO REINFORCE KEY MESSAGES

To cause *long-term* change, you'll need *long-term* communications. For instance:

1. Pre-communication questions, to find your people's key objectives and concerns.
2. Pre-communication tasters, to whet people's appetite for the change.
3. Your main communications, tailored to address the objectives and concerns you uncovered earlier.
4. Relentless, disciplined, focused follow-up communications, such as:
     Delivering weekly updates.
     Sharing success stories.
     Institutionalizing a coaching program.
     Publicizing early wins.
     Hosting regular meetings, for all relevant groups.
     Seeking feedback, both formal and informal.
     Stimulating water-cooler conversations.
     Selecting and training-up mentors.
     Delegating important follow-up roles to your best people.

REINFORCE MESSAGES THE RIGHT NUMBER OF TIMES

Follow-up is clearly important. But how much should you do? How many times should you tell them?

Well, like a bald man who's washing his face – believe me, I worry a lot about this – there's no right time to stop. But you can be sure of one thing: you will *definitely* have to communicate it more than once.

And, of course, people will need constant reminders and reassurance from you. If they don't get it right first time, encourage them. Ask how you can help them change. After all, I've yet to see a parent say to their toddler who stumbles when taking their first step: "Listen son, you're clearly not a walker". So:

1.   For communications you've recently delivered but didn't follow-up: follow them up! Ask people how they're progressing, offer help, share successes, and build momentum.
2.   For all your future communications, prepare both the communication *and* follow-up beforehand, not just the communication. And then keep following-up until things stick.

You would *never* buy a house with a credit card.

And you'll *never* cause long-term change with one communication.

Build Your Snowball: Cause Long-Term Change, not a Short-Term Blip

To bring about *long-term* change, you have to deliver *long-term* (not one-off) communications:

1. Find people's objectives/concerns.
2. Give them early tasters, to warm them up.
3. Deliver communications tailored to address their objectives/concerns.
4. Follow-up relentlessly, until it sticks.

24

When you want to use the best communication channel to get a quick "yes"

In soccer, one of the most frustrating things is to work hard to get an easy goal-scoring opportunity, only for the striker to shoot wide with just the goalkeeper to beat. All that work, time and energy invested in getting the opportunity . . . totally wasted by a needless mistake when it mattered.

Similarly, with communication, you don't want to invest lots of work, time and energy into creating persuasive content, only to "shoot wide" by choosing the wrong channel to communicate it. For instance:

- One-way information downloads on a conference call would often have been better as an email.
- Lengthy emails would often have been better as a conversation.
- Formal presentations to many would often have been better as a conversation with the main decision maker.

One way to choose the best channel is to "Good Grief" your options. This means giving each possible channel two scores out of 10, to show:

- Good – how likely that channel is to produce best results (where 10 is best); and
- Grief – how much grief this channel is likely to bring you in terms of cost, time, hassle and your hatred of it (where 10 is worst, because it's maximum grief).

Both are important. If it isn't *good*, it won't work. If there's too much *grief*, you won't want to do it.

For example, let's assume you have an unpopular message to communicate. A conference call might score (3, 4):

- 3 out of 10 for "good", because it's unlikely to produce the desired impact: delivering an unpopular message in this impersonal way won't engage; and

- 4 out of 10 for "grief", in that it's not much grief for you: you sit in your office, deliver the message, put the phone down and get on with your day.

So, given that a conference call is unlikely to work, let's look at alternatives by "Good Grief-ing" other channels. The following table shows scores you might allocate. (There's no "right or wrong". You decide what's right for you. These scores are just an illustration).

Channel	Good	Grief	Reasons
Conference call	3	4	As above.
Group email	2	1	Easy to write (no grief), but won't lead to good outcomes because it's so impersonal.
Presentation	6	9	Much more likely to work because of the face-to-face element, so a higher "good" score. But if you hate making presentations, or would feel awkward delivering this one, there'll be lots of grief.
Round-table dialogue	8	2	Much more likely to work. It's face-to-face, allows time for peer-to-peer discussion and for you to take immediate action in response to points raised. Also, there's not much grief: this option is less formal, easier to prepare for, and more consultative.
Video conference	4	5	Probably more likely to work than a conference call or group email (hence the higher "good" score) but less so than a presentation or round-table because there's no "live" face-to-face. This option is probably more grief than all the previous options (except the formal presentation you were dreading), because the others are easier.
Series of individual face-to-face discussions	10	10	This option is the most likely to work, because you can deal with everyone's questions instantly. However, it's the highest grief because it will take ages to do.
Writing a presentation for a colleague to deliver	1	10	Not good (it doesn't come from you) but lots of grief (you still have to write it... and then deal with everyone's fury after it).

You want the closest to (10, 1), in that this option is most likely to work, whilst bringing you minimal grief. Here, the round-table option is clearly best (not surprisingly, verbal will usually beat written) though, if you hadn't applied "Good Grief", you might have delivered the message during your weekly conference call.

And, of course, you don't have to choose just one option. For instance, in this example, you might:

1. Have a couple of individual face-to-face discussions with influential people (this might be worth the extra "grief", because getting them on-side early will make the rest easier).
2. Then, host a round-table discussion with everyone.
3. Follow-up with a group email, to make the message "official".
4. After a couple of weeks, host a video conference/conference call to take questions, share successes, remove concerns and so on.

And, because no business book is complete without a two-by-two matrix, here's how it looks visually:

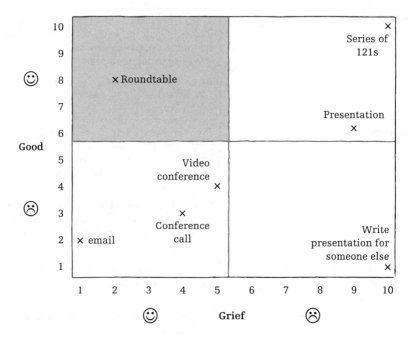

You can see how your best options are bunched top left. Sometimes, depending on its importance, it might be worth the extra grief involved and going top right.

Equally importantly, bottom right instantly shows what you *shouldn't* be doing.

Two final points:

Firstly, whatever channel(s) you use, make sure you get your title right or you won't engage them. Call anything "update" and it's not going to draw the crowds (this is really important; the next chapter shows how to do it).

And secondly, you'll find "Good Grief" is also useful when choosing between alternatives. For example, once salespeople see that cold-calling often scores (1, 10) and that word-of-mouth scores (10, 1), they never cold-call again. A blessing for everyone!

Without "Good Grief", it's all too easy to use the channel you're in the habit of using. But that might be a big mistake for certain messages; a bit like shooting wide with just the goalkeeper to beat.

Build Your Snowball: Use the Best Communication Channel to Get a Quick "Yes"

Use "Good Grief" to help choose your best channel(s), where:

- Good shows how likely that channel is to work; and
- Grief shows how horrible – costs, time, hassle – it is.

You want lots of the former and none of the latter.

25

When you want to create titles that instantly grab people

At my daughter's nursery, misbehaving children used to be put on the Naughty Mat. But the nursery felt this name sent out the wrong vibe – "Child, you're naughty". So, they now call it the Thinking Mat – "Sit there and think what you could do better next time".

This simple change has shifted the children's mindset about being on it – they sulk less and are ready to come off it sooner. Just because they changed its name.

You see, to persuade people, titles are critical. They help you engage people early. They set the tone for what follows. I touched on titles in chapter 1, but they're so important, it's worth spending a bit more time on them here.

When you think about it, you know titles are an essential part of communication. They're the first things people see. Newspapers employ experts to write headlines. Advertisers and publishers know a poor title destroys sales.

But, despite titles' importance, people rarely spend much time thinking about them. Their titles usually merely *describe* the content: "Departmental conference", "Our credentials", "Q2 review" and the like.

Don't believe me? Check your inbox. Let me guess: you've received emails called:

- "FYI"
- "Miscellaneous"
- "RE:"
- "Update"

They don't make you leap to open them, do they?

And it's not just emails. I mean, when slide one of a presentation says "Last month's results", you're not exactly itching to see slide two.

Or, when you have a conference call at 9am called "Update", you don't wake up that morning thinking "Yes. It's today!"

Uninspiring, boring titles set the tone for uninspiring, boring communications. It's hard enough to get a "Yes" without turning people off before you've even started speaking.

HOW TO CREATE ENGAGING TITLES

Fortunately, there's a simple, effective remedy. Add an audience-benefit to the title (or subtitle) and you change the context entirely. For instance, would you rather receive communications called:

- "Departmental conference" or "Ensuring next year's even better"
- "Our credentials" or "Where we can bring you most value"
- "Q2 review" or "Q3 preview: Ensuring we surge ahead"

See how it works? Better titles instantly transform other people's – and *your* – mindset about the communication.

Here's how to write them:

1. Turn your title into a benefit (use chapter 17's "Why That's Good Game" to help you).
2. Create a new title which includes this benefit. If it helps, use one of these formats:

Title format	Example
How to BENEFIT	How to save time.
An ADJECTIVE way to BENEFIT	A simple way to save time. (Depending on your topic, instead of "simple", use "guaranteed, cheap, pleasant, risk-free" and so on).
VERBing you BENEFIT	Helping you save time. (Instead of "helping", you could use "ensuring, easing, reducing, simplifying, magnifying" and so on).

3.   Decide whether the title should be either:
     The main title
     This makes the benefit prominent.
     For example, remember John in chapter 1? His original email title was
         "Figures". We changed it to "Making sure you get paid on time this month".
     Beware though: working the benefit into a main title can make it too long
         or too vague, or – when it's an email – look like spam. So, instead, you
         could put it in:
     A subtitle
     This time, you keep the original title as your main title and add a benefits-
         rich subtitle – "Communication Masterclass: Achieve amazing things
         every time you speak".

Of course, this advice relates to all your titles, not just the main one at the top. After
all, you don't want to open a document enticingly titled "How to inspire everyone",
only to find sections called "Background", "About us", and "Our process".

And it's also important that your introductions build on your engaging titles, to keep
people hooked (see the next chapter for how to do this).

Using effective titles is one of those things that sounds really obvious and you'd
imagine everyone would do it. One quick look at your inbox will show you they
don't (and one quick look at your Sent Items will show whether you do.)

**Build Your Snowball: Create Titles that Instantly
Grab People**

To secure early engagement, find the most persuasive benefit (to the
recipient) of your communication, and say it at the start. So, for
conversations, this will appear in your first 1–2 sentences; for other
communications, in your title and/or subtitle.

26

When you want to write eye-catching introductions

Every time you communicate, you want people to engage with you instantly. This gives you a much better chance of getting them to do what you want. This short chapter will help you do this very quickly. Let me explain . . .

Imagine that you work in Marketing, and want to share your new plans with the sales director. Which introduction would she prefer?

"Here's our Marketing plans for next year"; or

"I know you're keen to improve the performance of every one of your team, to reduce your dependence on a handful of superstars. We have a new approach to help ensure this happens. I want to show you how it will work, by running through our Marketing plans for next year."

The second is clearly much more compelling. It starts with *her* agenda, not yours (in fact, your agenda – the plan – isn't mentioned until the end of your introduction). This makes it much more likely to secure *her* buy-in.

Changing your introductions in this way is another of these ideas that should always happen, but rarely does. Don't believe me? Check your company's website and brochures and note how many paragraphs begin with the word "We", "Our" or your company's name. These are examples of *your* agenda, not the recipients'.

USE THE 4Ws TO CREATE POWERFUL INTRODUCTIONS

My 4Ws approach is a simple way to create better introductions. Using the Marketing example above to explain each W:

What they want – To improve every salesperson's performance
Why they want it – To reduce dependence on the superstars
We can help – "We can help"
What I'm discussing – Here's my Marketing plan

Does the 4Ws secure immediate buy-in? Well, check out the first paragraph of this chapter. Did it work?

To help you see where you might use the 4Ws, let's look at a couple more examples.

Giving an update following a recent restructure? Instead of "I'd like to update you with what's been going on", try:

*"Many of you have told me you're looking for more clarity following the recent changes, (**W**hat they want)*

*so we can all get on with our jobs more effectively and confidently. (**W**hy they want it)*

*So, that's what this meeting's all about. (**W**e can help)*

*I'm going to update you with what's been going on, and then . . . (**W**hat I'm discussing)"*

Running a workshop? Replace "Welcome to today's Excel Intermediate workshop" with:

"Every one of us needs more time, whether that's because we want to get more done, to finish work earlier, or just to make things more pleasant and simple. Today's session will help you achieve this. I'm going to show you how to use Excel to help you to . . ."

COMBINING GREAT TITLES WITH POWERFUL INTRODUCTIONS

The 4Ws works well alongside the previous chapter about intriguing titles, since a great title/introduction combo makes a very compelling start. For instance, one of my customers recently pitched for a multi-million dollar contract. Before I started to edit their proposal, the general format of every section was:

Our technology

We have cutting-edge technology that we can deploy the minute you agree to work with us. The key attributes of this technology, and the related benefits that it will bring, are . . .

With every section, we added a benefit to the titles, and a 4Ws introduction:

How our technology will increase your competitive advantage

Your #1 goal is to increase your competitive advantage, through developing a market-defining solution that your competition cannot match. The quicker and better you achieve this, the greater your return.

We can help you do this quickly, through our cutting-edge technology that we can deploy the minute you agree to work with us. The key attributes of this technology, and the related benefits that it will bring, are . . .

Notice how the 4Ws introduction (shown in italics) focuses *on their* agenda, not *yours?* Also, once your introductory paragraph is compelling, you often don't need to change what follows (I didn't alter the "our cutting-edge technology" paragraph) – great if you're short of time.

THE 4Ws EVEN WORKS AT HOME

Like many of this book's techniques, the 4Ws works at home too.

For example, it helped my daughter Megan become a school prefect. Part of the selection process involved students writing a letter explaining why they should be chosen.

When I asked her why she wanted to get the role, her first answer was "because it will look good when I apply for jobs". Sure, this was true; but it wasn't persuasive: it focused on her, not the school; plus every student would have said the same thing.

So, I showed her the 4Ws, and she wrote this introduction:

> *Dear Mr X,*
>
> *My name is Megan Bounds, from 10F, and I would very much like to become a prefect. I know it is an important role, and I feel as though I would be able to do it well. This letter explains what I think a prefect's job is, and examples of why I think I would suit this role.*
>
> <u>**Students want somebody to go to**</u>
>
> *I feel that being there for other students is one of the most important roles of a prefect. Students should have someone they feel they can go to when they're worried, or too nervous to go to a teacher.*
>
> *I can help with this, because I am used to being there for my younger siblings. I'm used to taking responsibility for them, and being there to answer their questions. I also . . .*

There aren't many techniques that both help companies win multi-million dollar contracts and teenagers become prefects. But 4Ws is one. Even better, it doesn't take long to do. That's got to be worth trying!

 Build Your Snowball: Write Eye-Catching Introductions

To ensure people buy-in early, shape your introductions around the 4Ws:

- **W**hat they want – their objectives.
- **W**hy they want it – the benefits they'll get from achieving these objectives.
- **W**e can help – state you can.
- **W**hat I'm discussing – now bring in your usual content.

27

When you want to use analogies to make your point

One of my customers recently told me:

> *"Our culture is stifling our management team. It's like owning a Ferrari, but driving it with the brakes on: it's a waste of an expensive, high-quality resource. We need to work out how to use our Ferrari better."*

Analogies like this explain the point you want to make (our management team is stifled) by likening it to something unrelated (driving a Ferrari with the brakes on). They're a great way to persuade, in that they:

- Increase understanding and buy-in – two key elements of persuasion.
- Often lead to less challenge – "Our management team is stifled" could easily be met with "No, it's not".
- Are especially useful when your message is not landing, is complex, unusual or just plain boring.

Analogies often work best when they're a bit "different" – a badly-driven Ferrari is a memorable picture – and/or refer to your audience's interests. For instance, telling a golf-loving boss that his approach is like "playing golf with an expensive tennis racquet" will resonate more than "this is costing too much".

HOW TO CREATE POWERFUL ANALOGIES

Technique 1 – use quotes or sayings
One approach is to use other people's analogies. For instance, to convince your business to invest *now* while there's spare cash, you might use John F. Kennedy's line: "The time to repair the roof is when the sun is shining."

And you can make it more powerful by following it with the foolishness of the reverse: "Our other option is to wait until it's raining, when we don't have as much money. We'd quickly wish we'd acted now."

If you know a good quote, use it. If not, there are thousands online. Just Google "quotations", choose a site, type in your topic and see what comes up.

Or, instead of using someone's comment, you could apply a well-known saying to your message. So, to encourage your colleagues to act quickly, you might use: "The early bird catches the worm. We need to act *now*."

Technique 2 – create your own analogies

The first technique can work well, but the analogies aren't original, so people might have heard them. So, in response to the "early bird" quote, somebody might say: "Yes, but the second mouse gets the cheese!" Also, you might just want to create your own. I certainly do.

There are three steps to creating analogies:

1.   Identify the message you want others to buy into.
2.   Create an analogy by thinking of a similar situation, in a different context.
3.   Add your recommendation/advice, so the analogy triggers a next step.

A quick example:

1.   My message: people's slides can be boring.
2.   My analogy: I think of somewhere I've seen good visuals, like TV weather forecasts.
3.   My advice: learn from the forecasters – give a couple of examples to make it real.

I would say this as follows:

> TV weather forecasters use visuals well. Their map changes to reflect what they're saying. The map has no writing on it, which would distract the viewer. Everything comes across clearly because of the combination of visuals and presenter.
>
> It should be the same when you use slides – reduce your words, use animations to clarify messages, and ensure your visuals and delivery complement each other.
>
> So, next time you're presenting, prepare like a weather forecaster, to make sure your slides enhance – not dilute – your message.

That analogy used a *better* version (the weather forecast) to show what people *should* be doing. Instead, I could compare current habits to a *worse* version, to motivate people to change:

> Have you ever tried to have a conversation while the TV's on too loud next to you? Even if the program's boring, it still absorbs most of your attention.
>
> It's the same with slides. If they're distracting – too wordy so people read them, or with spelling mistakes – you lose your audience. So my advice is . . .

One more example: do you remember puzzles like this from your childhood? If you had only 10 seconds to complete this puzzle, how would you do it?

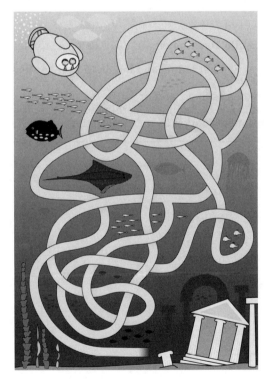

Start at the end and work backwards, yes?

It's the same when you're doing 30–60–90-day plans. Don't start at the 30. Like a maze, start at the end: know where you want to be in 90 days. Then, work backwards to see where you need to be after 60 days, to hit this 90-day target. Then, where you need to be in 30 to achieve your 60.

(Incidentally, of all the analogies I've made up, my favourite one is in the next chapter. It shows how to use Star Wars to help you structure communications).

Let's release the Ferrari

It's easy to communicate like you're driving a Ferrari with the brakes on. You have such valuable things to share, yet work pressures get in the way.

So make better use of your valuable insights. Analogies help you do this, by ensuring people embrace and act on your messages.

 Build Your Snowball: Use Analogies to Make Your Point

To help trigger understanding and buy-in to your key messages, use:

- Relevant quotes/sayings; and/or
- Your own analogy, by finding something to compare it to, and adding a recommendation so it causes action.

28

When you want to structure your communications so they're more persuasive

Star Wars changed many things about the film industry. It might also help change how you structure your communications.

Did you know, you don't have to watch any of the six Star Wars films? The titles tell you everything you need to know. To understand what I mean, you only need know that the goodies are called "Jedi" and the baddies are called "Sith", who work for the "Empire".

The six films are called:

1. *The Phantom Menace*
2. *Attack of the Clones*
3. *Revenge of the Sith*
4. *A New Hope*
5. *The Empire Strikes Back*
6. *Return of the Jedi*

In other words:

1. A baddie appears
2. There's a fight
3. The baddies win
4. There's hope for the goodies
5. But the baddies win again
6. And, finally, the goodies win overall

And that's it.

IF STAR WARS CAN DO IT, SO CAN YOU

And why's this relevant when you want to persuade someone? Well, they need to be able to follow your thought process. This means you need a clear, interesting structure.

So, like Star Wars, let your titles tell the story. Writing them *before* you write your content helps you flow smoothly from topic to topic. For example, if you were launching a new initiative, your titles could be:

- Times are getting harder
- And it's costing us money
- So, we looked at three options
- Option X was too risky
- Option Y was too expensive
- Leaving Option Z as the clear way forward
- So, our next steps are . . .

THREE QUICK STEPS, TO EMBED THE "STAR WARS WAY"

1. Always include "Next steps" as your final title. If you don't, there won't be any.
2. If it helps, use the four Ps to help create your titles (I used these in the above example):
    Position – The current situation is . . .
    Problem – And it's bad for us because . . .
    Possibilities – So our choices are . . .
    Propose – Therefore I propose our next steps are . . .
3. Once you have your titles, simply add the relevant content under each, and you have a well-structured, persuasive communication.

Build Your Snowball: Structure Your Communications So They're More Persuasive

To create a communication that flows, write your titles *before* your content, so you get the structure right. Then, put the relevant content under each one.

If it helps, use the four Ps (**P**osition, **P**roblem, **P**ossibilities, **P**ropose).

29

When you want to pass an exam

The final two chapters in this section focus on two "yeses" all of us want at some point:

- A "yes" from an interviewer – the next chapter describes how to write a résumé that stands out amongst all the others out there.
- A "yes" from an examiner – this one shows the most effective, simplest, quickest way of passing an exam.

Before I started doing what I do now, I used to teach accountants how to pass their professional exams (bit of a career change, I know). And these exams aren't easy. Many students, who'd sailed through exams all their lives, suddenly came unstuck with these, despite working harder than ever before.

I found that they almost always had enough knowledge to pass. But they didn't know how to maximize their marks given the knowledge they had.

I wanted to make it easier for them, so I spent years working out the best way to maximize marks. And it worked very well: I taught national prize winners; and my pass rates were much higher than national averages.

Here's what I found to be the best way to approach exams (I'm assuming here that they're written exams, not multi-choice ones).

FOCUS ON THE MARKER

Many students believe markers think of them as individuals. They don't.

I used to mark for one of the accountancy exams. It was hard work. I had 400 identical papers to mark, to a very high standard, with a very tight timeline, during the Christmas vacation.

I *never* once thought "I hope this particular person passes more than I wanted the others to." I just rigorously, fairly, dispassionately applied the marking guide to what was in front of me.

Given this, you have to help the marker give you as many marks as possible, by doing such things as:

- Use sub-headings that contain the same words as the requirement. This makes it easy for him to tie your answers to his marking guide.
- Ensure your writing is legible. If it isn't, you won't get marks. This means you have to practise writing neatly quickly. Believe me, the skill of speedy neatness doesn't suddenly appear in the exam room.
- Start a new paragraph every time you make a new point. Use short paragraphs with a blank line in between them. Bite-sized chunks are easier to mark quickly.

READ THE REQUIREMENT FIRST

The requirement shows what the examiner wants. Nothing else does. Therefore, read it first, before all the paragraphs of information they give. There are lots of benefits in doing this:

- A common examiner complaint is that people don't answer the question that was asked. Reading the requirement first helps stop this happening.
- You can often answer some requirements without having to read the text (see the next point for how to do this).
- When you do read the text, you know which bits are relevant to the requirement, so spot them more quickly.

A lot of students struggle with this, saying "but I want to read top to bottom, not bottom first."

I found the best way to persuade them was by setting a 10 Minute Power Test. I gave them five pages packed with detailed statistics, complex charts, lengthy paragraphs and unfathomable phrases, and 10 minutes to answer the question.

The room would go quiet for a few minutes, as they worked through this complicated mass of tedium. I swear I could sometimes feel their hatred building toward me.

And then someone would laugh, and say "oh this is easy". They'd seen the requirement at the bottom of Page 5 said "Write your name (100 marks)".

GET EASY MARKS FIRST

The dispassionate marker doesn't care what you find easy or hard. If you write something that's on the marking scheme, you'll get the marks. Therefore, always do the easy questions first. For example, imagine a question with this requirement:

> ### Requirement
>
> (a) In the above text, what are company X's main strengths? (4 marks)
> (b) Produce a six-month cashflow using the figures in paragraphs 3 and 4. (4 marks)
> (c) List four things a company may spend money on, and why. (8 marks)

Here, you would do part (c) without even reading the detailed paragraphs. Do this well, you might score the 50% you need to pass this entire question.

This approach means that you pick up most marks per minute at the beginning:

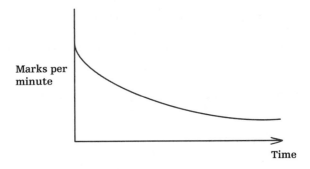

BREAK THE REQUIREMENT DOWN INTO BITS

Another common examiner complaint is that people don't answer *all* the questions asked. In the above example, where I suggested doing part (c) first, this actually had two elements to it:

- List four things a company may spend money on.
- And why.

It would be very easy to not see "And why", and throw away half the marks.

MAXIMIZE YOUR MARKS BY SEEING THINGS FROM DIFFERENT VIEWPOINTS

Exams often ask you to comment on something. These questions can be tricky to answer well, so I devised this approach that my students said helped them pick up lots of marks very quickly:

- Define it
- Give an example
- Say a good thing about it
- Say a bad thing about it
- Mention people affected by it
- Say how they're affected – good and bad

So, in answer to "Why is marketing important to a business?", the answer might start like this:

"Marketing" is all the activities a company undertakes to trigger interest in its products and services. Examples include:

- *The messages it sends to the marketplace – about a company's values, products etc.*
- *The channels it chooses for those messages – advertising, PR and so on.*
- *How marketable the product is – its price/value ratio and brand etc.*
- *Its use of social media.*

Marketing is essential in that it entices existing and potential customers to want to know more. This starts/continues the process of convincing them to buy.

But marketing has its problems. It can be very expensive. The return is often not immediate, or measurable.

And, because it can be hard to measure, it can be virtually impossible to know which methods are working. This might mean companies continue to invest in loss-making activities.

Marketing is also important to a business because of its impact on different types of people. For instance . . .

See how this approach helps you score marks quickly? This is because you now have black and white steps to answering gray, hard-to-start questions.

STOP ON TIME

One of the most common reasons people failed accountancy exams was because they got their timing wrong. Note that 20% of the marks should take 20% of the time. Put another way: if you spend 90% of your time on 5% of the marks, you won't have enough time left to get sufficient marks to pass.

Imagine that someone stopped doing their question on time, but you didn't. Look at the disastrous shaded area below . . .

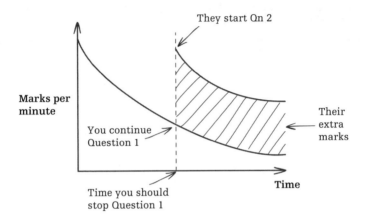

PREPARING IN THE RIGHT WAY

Three quick tips about preparing:

1. On the day, you have to answer *questions*. So, the best preparation is to practise *questions*. This is very different than simply learning the manual (which is like practising for a driving test by reading the Highway Code, but never once sitting behind a steering wheel).
2. If you're a "morning person", revise in the morning. I used to *despise* setting the alarm 90 minutes earlier, but I used to *love* that doing so saved me three hours in the evening. Even better, I'd done 90 minutes high-quality revision while other students were asleep. The things you cling to when you're revising!
3. Keep revision as interesting as possible. There's so much support now – podcasts, guides, journals, helplines – that you can choose the ones that best suit you. If you don't, and start to find it depressingly boring, you'll quickly start looking at your watch thinking "only 50 minutes to go to my next break . . . only 49½ minutes to go . . . only 49¼ minutes to go . . ."

Build Your Snowball: Pass an Exam

To give yourself the best chance of passing exams, you want to make it easy for both:

- The marker – use short paragraphs, clear headings, legible writing; and
- You – read the requirements first, do the easy bits next, stop on time and prepare properly.

30

When you want to get a job interview

When I left university, like many students, I didn't have a job. I was also – again, like many students – totally broke, so was living with my parents.

While I was still job-hunting, I remember watching my Dad review applications for a very senior position in his office. And I was *amazed* – and a bit gutted, to be honest – how quickly he reviewed people's résumés that they'd taken ages to write.

I mean, he read everything in there, and treated all the résumés fairly. But it was all just so *quick*. And it struck me how a recruiter's first read-through is often a filtering exercise, which puts people into one of three groups – extremely impressive; definitely not; everyone else.

Twenty years on, and I've helped hundreds of people secure senior jobs by ensuring their résumé goes into the first group. This chapter contains my top tips to help you do this. To make things as "real" as possible, I've included "before and after" excerpts of Carl's résumé (he's one of my customers) whose revised résumé led to an interview panel saying it was the best they'd ever read and that it "was like reading a story".

START WITH THE EMPLOYER'S NEEDS, NOT YOUR BACKGROUND

You want to grab attention from line one. This means focusing on the employer, not you. For example, Carl's original résumé began:

An outstanding and resilient NHS commissioning professional, with strategic and operational experience in both primary and secondary healthcare services and a reputation for de-mystifying complex data to effect change, Carl brings a proven record of delivering major savings and performance improvement across multiple trusts and levels of care.

We changed this to:

The ability to deliver *measurable outcomes* is more important than ever. Carl has a proven track record of helping the NHS achieve this, including:

- Transforming a £2m planned care budget overspend to operating a 2% surplus within a year.
- Delivering a 10% decrease in the number of patients waiting longer than 18 weeks for their treatment.
- Reducing GP consultations for common mental health disorders by 86,000 within a year.

FOCUS ON THE RESULTS YOU'VE *CAUSED*, NOT THE WORK YOU'VE *DONE*

Employers want to know you can deliver *results*. So focus on the *results* you've caused, rather than what you've done.

Did you notice how Carl's revised résumé did this in the previous example?

Originally he'd written these three points like this:

- Delivered major efficiency programs across community, primary, and secondary care.
- Worked extensively with GPs to embed new frameworks to improve patient outcomes and reduce unnecessary referrals.
- Jointly managed national programs locally, including implementing the Electronic Staff Record system across multiple trusts and hospitals and a national program to improve mental health outcomes.

TELL YOUR UNIQUE STORY IN A CLEAR, COMPELLING WAY

According to LinkedIn, most people sell themselves by using words such as "Extensive experience, dynamic, innovative, motivated, team player, results-oriented, great interpersonal skills, entrepreneurial".

Now people may well all have these characteristics. But, if *everybody's* saying them, they don't stand out. This is like the scene in my son Jack's favourite film *The Incredibles*, where Mrs. Incredible says "Everyone's special", to which her son replies "That's another way of saying 'no one is'".

Carl has some great, unique experiences, but he used to say things like:

> Carl was Regimental Sergeant Major of the Army's premier Field Hospital.

His résumé now reads:

> Carl's experiences – which include managing a £77m planned care budget and being part of the Army's executive team which was awarded the Wilkinson Sword of Peace – mean he knows how to deliver outcomes with measurable benefits.

LINK YOUR EXPERIENCES TO THEIR NEEDS

Carl used to describe himself using words like "outstanding and resilient". This is great if an employer wants someone outstanding and resilient. But it's often better to frame your qualities from the employer's point of view:

What the NHS needs...	Carl's relevant experiences...
Personal Resilience. The NHS's financial, political and demographic challenges mean you need leaders that sustain successful performance and well-being when facing adverse conditions.	During his time in the NHS, Carl has demonstrated that he is able to bounce back, and even grow, in the face of pressures and threats.

This personal resilience is due in part to his 24-years' service in the Armed Forces, in which Carl saw active service in the South Atlantic, Middle East, Balkans and the Mediterranean.

This experience has enabled Carl to trust his own judgement and intuition, and to take responsibility for himself. |

AND THE BEST ADVICE ABOUT YOUR RÉSUMÉ?

Don't rely on it.

Wherever possible (and it isn't always), do all you can to ensure your résumé isn't the first the decision maker hears of you. If you can, speak to them beforehand and/or ask a mutual contact to put in a good word.

After all, you'd rather their first thought was "Oh good, here's Carl's CV. I'm looking forward to reading this", and not "Just three more to go, then I'll have a break".

Build Your Snowball: Get a Job Interview

To write a résumé that sets you apart from the rest:

- Start with the employer's needs, not your background.
- When discussing your experiences, focus on the results you've *caused*, not the work you've *done.*
- Tell your unique story in a clear, compelling way.
- Link your experiences to their needs.

And, wherever possible, make sure your résumé *isn't* the first they hear of you.

SECTION D

Enjoy your job more

How to make work more fun

Chapter	When you want to ...
45	enjoy attending networking events
46	help people read your documents quickly
47	improve people's performance through observation and coaching
48	improve people's performance after annual reviews
49	improve people's performance when you delegate to them

WHY THIS MATTERS

One of the first questions I ask my new customers is whether they're having fun at work.

Almost none say "yes"; most replies being "no", "not really", "not at the minute", "I will do when X is finished" and "I will do when Y leaves me alone". I also get the occasional "it's going OK".

Admittedly, I probably have a skewed sample – after all, they've just asked me to help them with something. So, let me ask *you*.

Are *you* having fun at work?
When you wake up, do you look forward to your day?
Do you *know* it'll be great?

If you said three yeses, that's great (and very rare!). If not, this section will help you do something about it, by showing how to *enjoy* your dealings with others. As with the other sections, it contains lots of small chapters, so you can roll your snowball and pick up easy techniques as you go.

You go to work for thousands of days in your lifetime. You might as well really enjoy them. Let's look at easy ways to help you do so.

31

When you want to ensure everyone – including you – thinks you're great

To enjoy your job more, there's a question you absolutely *must* have a good answer to: *"What do you do?"* So how would you complete the sentence . . .

My job is to . . .

Most people answer this question with either:

- What they *are* – "I'm an accountant"; or
- What they *do* – "I prepare tax returns".

Neither *grabs* you, do they? And that's because people are much more interested in:

- What they *cause* – "I help people pay less tax".

Doesn't this person sound useful?! And I bet they *enjoy* their job too. They'll know the value they deliver to others. They'll be in demand. They'll probably be very successful. By sorting out their *inside* (how they feel about themselves), they now have a valuable *outside* (how others see them).

Weird, isn't it? It's the same accountant. They're just describing themselves more effectively now. Here's how you can do the same.

An "Elevator Pitch" can focus on one of three things:

(*For a quick reminder about AFTERs, see chapter 1).

The right-hand side is *by far* the most valuable. So, you should talk about that side more.

HOW TO ENSURE *YOU* THINK YOU'RE GREAT

Once you know to focus on the AFTERs you *cause*, you see examples of it everywhere:

- Disney talks about "making your dreams come true", not its cartoons.
- Kodak talks about your memories, not its photographs.
- Graham Gooch calls himself the England cricket team's "Run-making Coach", not "Batting Coach".
- And, for me, my job is to help people communicate better, not to be a consultant/author.

To create an AFTERs-rich Elevator Pitch, there are three elements:

1. The subject.
2. The verb.
3. The AFTERs.

Here are three examples, to show how the steps work.

	Example 1	Example 2	Example 3
1. The subject	I	This presentation	Our Department
2. The verb	help	will show	ensures
3. The AFTERs	people pay less tax	you how to deliver better results next year	our target market thinks we're better than the competition

Each is much better than the more traditional approach:

	I'm an accountant	This presentation is a review of last year	We're the Marketing Department

So, what's your Elevator Pitch?

1. The subject	I
2. The verb	
3. The AFTERs	

Compare this to your Elevator Pitch at the start of this chapter. Can you see how much more valuable you look now? Even though, just like the accountant above, you're still the same person.

Once you have an impressive AFTERs-rich Elevator Pitch, your next step is to find evidence that proves *to you* that it's right. For instance, think you're a Tax Reducer? Then identify:

- Examples of when you've saved people tax.
- The total amount of tax you've saved.
- Tax advice that others don't know.

And then work hard to get even better at delivering your AFTERs. For instance:

- Find new ways to increase tax savings.
- Give free advice about it.
- Keep at the forefront of your industry.
- Ask others for their tax-saving ideas.
- Publish white papers about saving tax.

. . . *anything* that keeps you as AFTERs-y as possible.

And, of course, AFTERs are also a great way to align your team with your vision. For example, Bev James, CEO of The Coaching Academy (the world's largest training school for coaches), told me that she uses AFTERs to remind her team why they do what they do. So, they no longer think of themselves as "coaches"; instead, they "help people achieve more than they thought they could". Imagine the power of having your whole team thinking like that.

HOW TO ENSURE *EVERYONE* THINKS YOU'RE GREAT

When I want to pay less tax, I'll go to someone who sees their role as a Tax Reducer, not as an Accountant.

When I want to grow my business, I'll go to a bank which talks about my Business Growth, not its Business Development Loans.

When I want to score more runs, I'll go to Graham Gooch, not to a batting coach (though even he might struggle to help someone who's blind in one eye).

In other words, once you've convinced yourself of the AFTERs you cause, it's relatively easy to convince *others*. You just need to mention your AFTERs every time it's appropriate – in conversations, meetings, networking events, interviews, presentations, documents, brochures, websites and so on.

HOW YOUR AFTERs-FOCUS IMPROVES YOUR COMMUNICATION

Once you realize your role isn't to *do* things but to *cause* things, your communications naturally improve:

A do-er thinks...	An AFTERs-causer thinks...
"What should this meeting *cover*?"	"What should this meeting *cause*?"
"What do I want to *say*?"	"What do I want them to *do*?"
"This session ends at 4pm."	"The session ends as soon as we achieve our goal."
"When building relationships, I think what they and I *do*."	"When building relationships, I think how can they and I help each other."

So, not only do AFTERs-causers feel valuable, they also communicate more quickly and effectively. They get more done. They have better relationships. They enjoy the ride more.

AND FINALLY . . .

So, having gone through all this, here are two big questions:

1. How do you describe yourself to *others*?
2. How do you describe yourself to *yourself*?

The more you focus on the AFTERs you *cause*, the more others will too – making you feel more valuable to them. And to you.

Build Your Snowball: Ensure Everyone – Including You – Thinks You're Great

Your role isn't to *do* things; it's to *cause* things.

Focus on the AFTERs you deliver – in other words, how people's *futures* are improved after working with you. The more you do this, the more they – and you – view you as essential.

32

When you want to build powerful relationships quickly

To enjoy your job, you want powerful relationships with great people. This drives *everything* – the quality of your conversations, the ease with which you get things done, your sense of fulfillment at work and home, and how successful you are. As Tony Robbins says: "People's lives are a direct reflection of the expectations of their peer group."

Given how important relationships are, you'll want to get them right. Fortunately, there are only three main things to focus on:

1. Know the right people.
2. See them the right number of times.
3. Have the right conversations with them.

1. KNOW THE RIGHT PEOPLE

Networking takes time. It's bound to, I suppose. After all, it's called net-*work*, not net-*wait-for-something-to-happen*.

So, to get best results when networking, spend the most time with people who have both the:

- Power to help you; and
- Desire to do so.

A simple way to evaluate your current network is to grade each of your main contacts' Power and Desire, and plot them on the following chart:

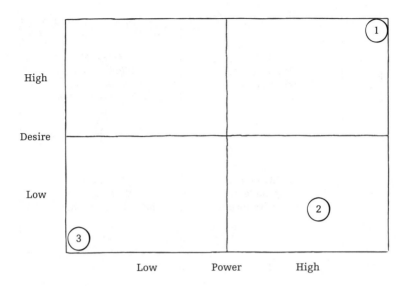

So, in my chart, **1** might be a CEO who thinks you're great (high power and desire); **2** might be a Board member who doesn't know you well (high power but low desire); and **3** could be the new part-time junior who doesn't know you at all (low both).

This chart helps show:

- The strength of your network – do most of your contacts have the power and/ or desire to help?
- What to do with each person on there.

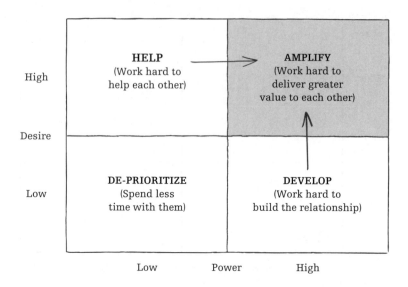

Three quick notes to help you:

1. The two arrows show the direction you want to go:
   Developing your relationships with "high power/low desire" builds their desire to help you.
   Your "low power/high desire" contacts could help by introducing you to their powerful contacts.
2. You'll notice I keep saying to work hard (as I said earlier, "it's called net-*work*").
3. The chart's real value is in *doing* it. If you've five minutes now, why not look at your contacts in your phone, and plot them on here? What patterns do you see? What are the strengths/weaknesses of your network? Do you spend time with the right people?

2. SEE YOUR CONTACTS THE RIGHT NUMBER OF TIMES

It's pretty obvious that you should see people the "right number of times". In fact, it's so obvious that – if work and life didn't get in the way – you wouldn't need this section.

But, unfortunately, work and life *do* get in the way. And when you're busy and your brain's full of all sorts of stuff, it's easy to forget to spend time with the people you should be seeing (or spend too long with those you shouldn't).

So, make it easier by inserting *recurring* diary reminders to speak to them. This means you never have to remember it yourself.

If it helps, use a KITE table (where KITE stands for **K**eep **I**n **T**ouch **E**very):

Name	KITE...
[The names of your key contacts, e.g. John Smith]	[How often you should speak to them – weekly, monthly, quarterly etc]

Then, group all the same types – e.g. the "monthlies" – in one recurring diary entry called "contact the following people: X, Y, Z". When the reminder comes up every month, just do what the diary says!

Some people feel KITE is over the top. And for you it might be. But, in my experience, these same people often also tell me "I really must speak to Mrs. X more often".

3. HAVE THE RIGHT CONVERSATIONS

I think my previous bank manager used to have a KITE table. Every month – without fail – he'd call to try and sell me something.

Hmmm . . . that's not relationship building; that's selling (these two are like oil and water – your business needs both, but they don't mix very well). In fact, it wasn't really "selling"; it was just annoying.

So, when you contact people, remember the Golden Rule of relationship building:

Always bring value

Or, if you prefer, make sure they think "I'm glad he called". There are lots of things you can do to achieve this:

1. Ask how you can help them.
2. Ask if they want you to send an article you saw/wrote that they'd find useful.
3. Ask how they/their family are.
4. Ask what they're working on; and, if appropriate, offer to help.
5. Introduce them to one of your contacts.
6. Publicize them in some way (for example, endorse them on LinkedIn).
7. Invite them to an event.
8. Send them a book you think they'd find helpful.
9. Give advice if they want it.
10. Refer to something they told you previously.

There are loads. You'll notice quite a few include the word "ask" – the next chapter has more on how to do this well. You'll also notice *none* involve shoving banking products down someone's throat!

One final point: these don't take much time/effort, but all bring huge value to your contacts, and therefore to you. Even better, you can leverage the ones you choose. For instance, one month, you might share the same article with lots of different people. Each of them thinks "I'm glad he called", and it wasn't at all onerous for you.

In many ways, this is one of the most important chapters in the book. Build great relationships with great people, and success becomes inevitable. What one action could you take, to be even better at it?

**Build Your Snowball: Build Powerful
Relationships Quickly**

There are three important steps:

1. Know the right people, who have both the power and desire to
   help you.
2. Diarize to see them the right number of times, using **KITE** – **K**eep
   In **T**ouch **E**very.
3. Have the right conversations, such that you *always* bring them
   value.

33

When you want to get things right first time

"Give me some Rules of Thumb about communication that I can follow every time. Without thinking."

So said one of my customers recently. I asked what areas he was most interested in.

Him: Well, when I'm making a formal presentation, should I use PowerPoint or not?

Me: *I don't know. It depends what your audience wants. Your best bet is to ask how they want you to deliver it.*

Him: OK, but if I *do* use PowerPoint, should I send the slides in advance, or take everything with me on the day?

Me: *It depends. I suggest you ask if they want to see something upfront.*

Him: And, should I start my presentation with background information, to set the scene?

Me: *It depends. Many people don't care, but some do. I'd ask them if they want it. And, if so, ask which bits they're most interested in.*

Him: And who should present it? The best presenters on my team? Me? The people who'll be doing the work?

Me: *It depends. I suggest you ask . . .*

Him (interrupting me): This is *exasperating*. I'm looking for Rules of Thumb. And you keep saying it depends.

Me: *Can't you hear the Rule of Thumb? Ask.*

The best way to give people the information they want is to *ask* what information they want. Contact them beforehand, and say:

1.   What do you want me to cover?
2.   What do you *not* want me to cover?
3.   What do you think are the most positive aspects of this topic?
4.   What do you think are the most concerning?

Answers 1 and 2 tell you what to talk about.

Answer 3 – their positives – could well appear in your title/subtitle to grab attention early (so, if their answer was speed, your subtitle might be something like "A quick resolution to X").

Answer 4 gives you vital information about their concerns, which you *must* address during your communication. If you don't, they'll still be concerned – no good for either of you (chapter 53 shows how to reduce concerns).

There are other questions you can ask too of course, but I find these first four are a great start. Others that uncover useful information include:

- Who else will see my communication? What will they want me to include?
- Does this topic relate to everyone, or just certain people?
- Would you prefer a formal PowerPoint presentation, or an informal discussion?
- How long would you like me to speak for?
- Will there be a Q&A session? If so, would you prefer questions during, or at the end?
- . . . and so on.

These questions will help. But get the balance right between getting guidance and getting on their nerves. If in doubt, it's often worth asking one too many questions, rather than one too few. After all, if you don't ask, you're guessing, which can easily go spectacularly wrong.

TO FIND LOTS OF GOLD, DIG DEEP

If you were digging for gold, and could use either a pneumatic drill or a spade, which would you choose?

The drill, right? It's easier, and would hit gold more quickly.

The problem though is that the drill digs *too* quickly. So, yes, you'll reach gold earlier, but you'll then keep hurtling downwards, missing most of it. Contrast that with a spade. It'll take longer but, when you hit gold, you'll dig sideways along the vein. So, the spade is harder work, but you'll get *lots* more value from using it.

It's the same when asking questions. Treat their answers like *gold*. Don't hurtle past with a speedy pneumatic drill, but use a spade to dig deeper into what they say, using:

- Questions – why, when, how, what; and/or
- Digging phrases – "tell me more", "please expand on that", "anything else?"

So, imagine you're preparing a presentation for your Board. You call a Board member to ask for guidance. Your spade-digging may go something like this:

> You: What would like me to cover? (This is the first question from earlier.)
> *Her: Just give us a quick update.*
> You: Sure. What in particular do you want updating on?
> *Her: The impact when we move into Belgium.*
> You: Why Belgium?
> *Her: Because it's our focus now.*
> You: Why's that?
> *Her: Because it's going to be our biggest market.*
> You: Really? Why?
> *Her: [more detail]*
> You: So, what aspects of my initiative do you think are most relevant to your aims for Belgium?
> *Her: [they reply]*
> You: And, given all this, is there anything you don't want me to cover at the Board meeting? (This is the second question from before.)

This looks like a lot of work. But it isn't. In fact, this interchange would only take a few minutes. But imagine if you *hadn't* asked any questions. You just *wouldn't* have known what was wanted.

Or, imagine you hadn't used your spade to dig along the gold. You'd have thought she wanted an "update" and would have missed the key focus was Belgium.

(A useful aside: in media interviews/parliamentary questions, people often see the questions they'll be asked in advance, so they prepare for them. But they *don't* see the follow-up questions, which often provide the real challenge and insight.)

This chapter has led us to the following indisputable conclusions:

- Ask no questions – bad idea: it means you're guessing everything.
- Asking 1–2 questions – bad idea: it means you're guessing nearly everything. Even worse, you might feel you've done your research and are basing your content on "facts", which you're not.
- Spending time digging with your spade – great idea: it leads to better, shorter, more successful communications (the next chapter shows you how to ensure they're interesting too).

Build Your Snowball: Get Things Right First Time

To ensure you impress people with your first attempt:

- Ask people what they want you to focus on.
- Dig deep with their answers, so you – and they – understand what they *really* want.
- Prepare your communication based around their deep answers (which might be very different from their first ones).

34

When you want to deliver interesting presentations that impress everyone

Most presentations sure are dull, aren't they? Awful slides, monotonous delivery, zero engagement, some – as we discussed in the last chapter – even discuss the wrong thing!

This means it should be pretty easy for yours to stand out. This chapter shows a very simple way to ensure they do.

Firstly, since you want to interest *others*, start by thinking about what *others* find interesting. For instance, they like:

- Interactivity – pretty much everyone would rather join in a dialogue than listen to someone talk *at* them
- Interesting stories
- Brevity
- Fun
- To learn something new
- Good visuals
- To achieve something important
- Interesting quotations
- Variety

Then expand this list by adding the *opposite* of what people hate. For instance, since people hate word-y slides, using "sparse slides" would make you more interesting. Your list might now include:

- Sparse slides (not word-y)
- Short paragraphs (not long)
- Clear headings (not too few, or too boring)

- Minimal background information, especially at the start (avoids the tedious 10-slide scene-set).
- Using the right channel (don't give a presentation if a chat's all that's needed).
- Relevant (thus avoiding the dreaded "why am I here?").

The next step is to think what you could do, to be more like the list. For instance, if you want your presentations to be more interactive, you could ask more questions, or put people in pairs to discuss topics. Your list might now look like this:

People like... (the theory)	Actions you could take to be more like this (the practice)
Interactivity	• Ask questions. • Put people in pairs/groups, to discuss key points. • Ask somebody else to deliver part of the session.
Stories	• Prepare them in advance. Practise, test and refine them until they're good. • When one works well, use it with other audiences.
Brevity	• Everything in chapter 1, especially focusing on what you want people to *do* afterwards. • Remove as much content as possible.
Fun	• Games, quizzes, icebreakers, jokes, energizers (the next three chapters give some examples of these). • Think what you've enjoyed when in an audience, and use something similar. • Involve the "fun" people in your team.
To learn something new	• Bring your own original thoughts. • Ask experts for their advice. • Research.
Good visuals	• Use some. There are all sorts – pictures, flowcharts, tables, graphs – *anything* that isn't just words. • When it matters, use professional designers.
To achieve something important	• Position your advice so it's in their interest – "You want to achieve X. This will help you". • Ask what's stopping them progressing, and help them remove it.
Interesting quotations	• Use quotations you like. • Ask colleagues for quotes that they like. • Use Google to find good quotation websites, input your key words and see which quotations come up. For any you like, learn more about the author, source and context so you can "tell the story".

People like... (the theory)	Actions you could take to be more like this (the practice)
Variety	• Check your communication isn't all the same (e.g. 15 consecutive slides of bullet points). If it is, insert something from this table into the middle of that section. • Ask yourself "When will they be bored?" and make suitable changes.
Sparse slides	• Remove as many words as possible, or • Start with a blank slide and write only your key words on it. • Use interesting layouts, e.g. a box around each, a flowchart etc.
Short paragraphs	• Press "return" more often! • Leave a blank line between paragraphs.
Clear headings	• Have at least one heading per page. • Use interesting headings, not the usual "Background", "FYI" and "About us". • With long sections, group information into mini-sections, and put a sub-heading above each.
Minimal background information	• Ask them what background information they want to see. • Shorten your background information. • Move some/all of it to an appendix (or the bin).
Use the right channel	• Use the best channel (this might not be the one you usually use). • Ask people how they'd like you to deliver your message to them. • Consider a combination of channels. For instance, turn a 1-hour conference call into (i) a briefing chat (ii) a 20-minute conference call, and (iii) a follow-up email.
Relevant	• Ask beforehand: "What would you like me to cover?" • Share your proposed structure beforehand, and ask for feedback before you complete your prep.

This table isn't exhaustive. But it's a good start. In fact, it's such a good start, you might think "How on earth am I going to do all that?"

Well, you don't have to do "all that". But, to be more interesting, you'll have to do more than none of it.

So, identify 1–2 things from the right-hand column that would make a huge difference and be relatively easy to do. Do them; fine-tune them; then, once they're working, incorporate another 1–2 and so on.

Or, of course, you can set your sights higher, and incorporate all the techniques in this chapter. A good example of someone who's done this is Charlie Lawson, who is the UK National Director of BNI, the world's largest referrals and networking organization. He uses pretty much every tip in the table, and is an excellent trainer. I asked him what his favourite one was. He said:

> *"When you told me people learn most when I'm not talking! They like inter-activity. They like thinking. They like applying my ideas to their situation.*
>
> *This means I'm now always looking for opportunities to shut up. They love it. They learn more. And it's easier for me. So, everyone wins!"*

 Build Your Snowball: Deliver Interesting Presentations that Impress Everyone

To become a more interesting communicator:

1. List the communication techniques that you know others find interesting (e.g. interactivity, stories).
2. Identify simple actions you could take, to be more like this list (e.g. asking questions, writing and practising stories).
3. Incorporate (at least) 1–2 of these actions into your communication style.

35

When you want to use "word pictures" to help people remember things

Here's a great way to help people remember your key messages. I'm going to use the seven drivers of shareholder value as my example:

1. Sales growth.
2. Profit margin.
3. Cost of capital.
4. Investment in working capital ("working capital" being a business's short-term assets/liabilities that help it run smoothly. It's like oil in a machine – too much is expensive; too little, and the machine breaks down).
5. Investment in fixed assets.
6. Tax.
7. Competitive advantage period.

So, my question: If I asked you to memorize all seven, such that you could recall them weeks from now, how would you do it?

I guess you'd read the list a few times until it stuck? But that's boring, takes ages, and won't stay in your long-term memory. You'd remember some tomorrow, but in a week?

One of my previous jobs involved teaching accountants how to pass their professional exams. This list was one of the many lists they had to remember. And, as you've just seen, it's pretty forgettable – especially in a pressurized exam room. So, instead of learning this list, I asked them to imagine something very different:

1. Think of a sailing boat with three sails: one small, one medium and one huge.
2. Marge Simpson is driving the boat.
3. She's wearing a red cap with the price tag attached.
4. The boat isn't in the sea – it's floating on oil in a container.
5. A baby donkey is attached to the side of this oil container.
6. It's been attached by some tacks.
7. It has a tennis racket in its mouth.

Here's how the two lists are linked:

1. Three growing sails = sales growth.
2. Marge Simpson = profit marge-in.
3. The cap with the price tag = cost of CAPital.
4. Oil = working capital.
5. Just as a baby pig is called a piglet, pretend a baby donkey ("ass") is an asset, fixed to the side = fixed asset.
6. . . . by tacks = tax.
7. You often hear the word "advantage" when watching tennis = competitive advantage period.

You're much more likely to remember this second list. My students did. And when it mattered: in the exam room. In fact, I met one of them recently for the first time in 10 years. He told me he could still remember it!

As well as being useful, "word pictures" are just more *fun* than a "word list", aren't they? I mean, which do you prefer?

So, when you've got a few key messages that people need to recall instantly, consider using a "word picture". The more unusual the pictures, the more impactful they are (just like the "don't think of a green hippo" idea).

Your lists don't need to be as long as my example. For instance, let's say you only want to remember three techniques from this book – think outside the box (chapter 37), have pit-stop meetings (chapter 7) and use BO to get a "yes" (chapter 18), you might use:

- A cardboard box with arms and legs (think outside the box).
- Standing on a Formula One car in the pits (pit-stop meetings).
- Spraying deodorant under his smelly armpits (BO).

As you can see, these can be pretty memorable.

Build Your Snowball: Use "Word Pictures" to Help People Remember Things

To help yourself/others remember a few points in a fun way:

- List the points.
- Link each one to an interesting visual.
- Group the visuals into one big picture.
- Share the picture with others.
- Ask them in a few days' time what they remember.

(If it will help you remember this list, why not create a word picture for it?)

36

When you want to use initials to help people remember things

Comedian Bob Monkhouse used to say presentation skills were all about your ABC and XYZ:

- **A**lways **B**e **C**onfident
- e**X**amine **Y**our **Z**ipper

Great advice!

Another example: my wife Emma read lots of baby books when Maia was born. But, when she had Tom nearly four years later, she didn't re-read one of them – *Secrets of the Baby Whisperer* – because she remembered it's advice about making things EASY:

- **E**at – when the baby wakes up, give her food.
- **A**ctivity – after the food, encourage her to do something.
- **S**leep – after the activity, put her to sleep.
- **Y**ou – when she's asleep, do something you want to do.

And one more example: when people ask me for an easy way to prepare communication, I tell them to RAMP it up:

- **R**esults – what you want the recipient to do afterwards (your Call To Action at the end).
- **A**FTERs – why they will be better off AFTER doing it (your engagement piece at the start).
- **M**echanism – how you're going to deliver the communication (email, meeting, presentation).
- **P**reparation – once you've done RAM, only then can you begin to prepare.

Initial letters help people remember lists, especially when the word is short, and relates to your message (like, this is an EASY way to look after your baby).

There are only four steps to creating these lists:

1. Identify your key words.
2. Highlight the initial letters.
3. Turn these initials into a word (use an online anagram generator if it helps).
4. If you can't find an anagram, find synonyms for your words, and repeat with the new initials.

To show what I mean by the last point, here's how I got to RAMP. I started off with:

- **D**o – what you want people to do afterwards.
- **B**enefit – why they'll benefit from doing it.
- **C**hannel – which communication channel you'll use.
- **P**reparation.

Now, no anagram generator is going to do much with the initials DBCP, so I thought of other words I could use instead:

- Do, objective, aim, result
- Benefit, AFTER, aid, help
- Channel, mechanism, process
- Preparation, create, write, narrative

And, from the various combinations of initials, I ended up with RAMP (it was either that or DAMN!)

Build Your Snowball: Use Initials to Help People Remember Things

Take the first letter of each of your key messages and make a single word with them.

Share this word with people, explaining each of your points within it. Then, reinforce the key word again and again, until it sticks.

And then again.

37

When you want to use games and activities to make your point

Here are three quick puzzles for you:

Puzzle 1
A blind beggar had a brother who died. What relation was the blind beggar to the brother who died? (The answer isn't "brother".)

Puzzle 2
Arthur lives with his parents in London.

Last week, while his parents were out, Arthur's next-door neighbour Sophie came round to spend the evening. At 8pm, she popped out to buy a newspaper.

Just then, two robbers broke into the house and, ignoring Arthur, stole the TV and computer.

Arthur had never seen the robbers before. They had no legal right to remove the goods. Yet he did nothing to stop them. In fact, he didn't even act surprised by what he saw.

Why not?

Puzzle 3
Colin went to a party and drank some of the punch. He then left early. Everyone else at the party who drank the punch subsequently died of poisoning. None of them had eaten or drunk anything else that could have poisoned them.

Colin didn't put anything in the punch after he drank it, nor did anyone else.

Why didn't he die?

How did you get on? The answers are "It was his sister", "Arthur was a baby", and "the poison was in the ice. Colin drank his punch before the ice had melted".

Top tip: things look different depending on your perspective.

Here's another one – join up the nine dots with four straight lines. The only rule: your pen can't leave the paper.

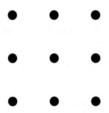

Need a clue? This puzzle is where the phrase "think outside the box" comes from.

Top tip: to come up with new ideas, think in new ways. Don't be constrained by your usual thought processes.

People like games and activities, as long as they're:

1. Fun.
2. Delivered at the right time – so not during a redundancy announcement, for example; and
3. Have a point, like the "Top tips" above.

So, since they're popular, include some. Use ones you've seen before. Search online for them. Ask people for recommendations.

As long as they tick these three boxes, they make your communications more enjoyable for everyone; which, of course, makes them more likely to work.

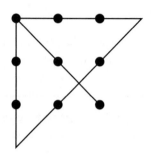

 Build Your Snowball: Use Games and Activities to Make Your Point

Use relevant games and activities to help people enjoy, understand and remember your messages.

When you *don't* bring messages to life, they're less memorable. This means you'll have to either:

1. Spend time reinforcing them; or
2. Accept the fact they'll be forgotten.

Now, there's two compelling reasons for doing this.

38

When you want to enjoy using PowerPoint

I can't recall ever seeing a chapter about *enjoying* PowerPoint before.

But it's important. If *you* don't enjoy it, how can you expect your audience to? As you know, PowerPoint has lots of negative connotations. For example, two phrases I often hear are:

"I don't feel comfortable making presentations."

"I use PowerPoint as a Comfort Blanket."

Which does beg the question: How rubbish must PowerPoint be as a *Comfort* Blanket, if everyone feels so *uncomfortable* using it? It's not a Comfort Blanket; it's a Habit Blanket.

Audiences *hate* sitting through tedious, same-y slides. Presenters hate delivering alongside them. So, here's a few simple guidelines to help you – and your audience – enjoy your slides.

1. GO TO POWERPOINT LAST, NOT FIRST

PowerPoint should be a tool to convey your thinking, not the way you think. So start your preparation by first identifying what you want your audience to do as a result of your presentation, then create good content. Then, and only then, open up PowerPoint.

This is much more likely to work than starting with "Right, what slides have I already got that I can use?"

2. USE THE VISUAL THING FOR VISUAL THINGS

PowerPoint is an excellent tool for communicating visual messages – graphics, charts and so on.

But it's a *terrible* way to communicate full sentences and reasoned arguments. You're better at those.

Either use visual, text-light slides; or detailed, text-heavy documents. Don't create something that tries to be both but ends up being neither.

3. MAKE YOURSELF SMILE

Use a visual that makes you smile. If you like it, your audience probably will. Either choose one you've seen before, ask your colleagues for suggestions, or find one online – it's easy to do: there are *thousands* of them.

4. PRESS "B" OR "W"

My favourite thing about PowerPoint: ensure your audiences look at you – not your slides – by blanking out the slides when you're talking. Press B (for black) or W (for white) to do this.

5. USE POWERPOINT SHORTCUTS

This helps you look polished when presenting. Two very useful ones are:

- Press the function key "F5" to start your presentation in show mode.
- Once in show mode, to jump to slide 8, press "8" and "enter". This is much better than pressing the "up" cursor 26 times.

6. CHAT, DON'T RANT

Most presenters and audiences prefer discussion to monologue. So, whenever you can, include discussion topics in your presentations.

Maybe have a slide that just says "discussion time", or a visual of people talking? Or, blank your slides (see #4) and ask a question to start a discussion – "So, how do you think this will impact us?" or "Before I carry on, does this idea seem sensible to you?"

7. UNCLUTTER YOUR SLIDES

Always remember that your slides should accompany – not duplicate – you. They mustn't tell the whole story, otherwise there's no point you being there. Only put key, simple, digestible words/visuals on your slides, for you to elaborate on (the next chapter shows you how to do this).

When you master this, it helps you stand out. Neil Fuller, who's been a Senior Executive at two global financial institutions, told me it's been a real differentiator for him:

> *"My presentations get things done. Now that I use my slides to enhance my presentations – rather than simply reading out the bullet points – people understand my messages, and act on them much more quickly. And, because most people don't present in this way, it helps me stand out from the crowd."*

8. AND, THE BEST ONE OF ALL?

I love using slides when they help my audience understand something. I *hate* using them when they're not needed, because they stifle discussion and thought.

So, whenever you can, *don't* use slides.

A POINT TO PONDER

Many years ago, there was no such thing as PowerPoint. If people wanted visuals, they used flipcharts. This often led to less words and better visuals because they were a hassle to create. They added to the audience experience.

Nowadays, it's so easy to put everything on slides that . . . well, people put everything on slides. And, to paraphrase Jeff Goldblum in *Jurassic Park* when he's advising against resurrecting dinosaurs . . . when asking yourself whether you should use all PowerPoint's capabilities, think "Just because you *could* doesn't mean you *should*".

Build Your Snowball: Enjoy Using PowerPoint

To help you and your audience enjoy your slides, always remember:

- Go to PowerPoint last, not first – starting there slows down your thinking.
- Use the visual thing for visual things – no full sentences on slides; only visuals.
- Make yourself smile – if you like it, they will.
- Press "B" or "W" – this blanks the screen.
- Use PowerPoint shortcuts.
- Chat, don't rant – whenever you can, engage in dialogue; don't just monologue.
- Unclutter your slides – make them easy to read.
- And, the best advice of all? Whenever you can, don't use slides.

39

When you want to create great visuals to enhance your message

Have you ever seen a slide like this?

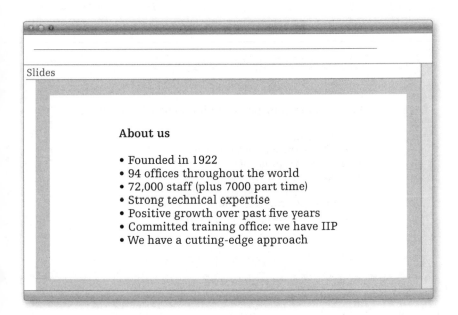

And have you ever thought: "This is *terrible*. It's boring. It isn't tailored to me. I just don't care."

Now two worrying questions:

1. Have *you* ever used wordy slides like this?
2. And what do you think your audience thought when you did?

Your slides should enhance your message, not dilute it. In fact, I've seen slides which actually *contradict* the message, like the one above: the "cutting-edge approach" doesn't extend to the slide design, apparently.

Fortunately, it's easy to transform these boring slides. There are six easy steps – my Slide Rules.

STEP 1: IMPROVE YOUR TITLE

This is a quick way to show your slides are useful. All you do is take your original title – in this case, "About us" – and ask yourself why it's interesting for the audience. In our example, assuming they want to know if you can help their colleagues enjoy their jobs more, a better slide would be:

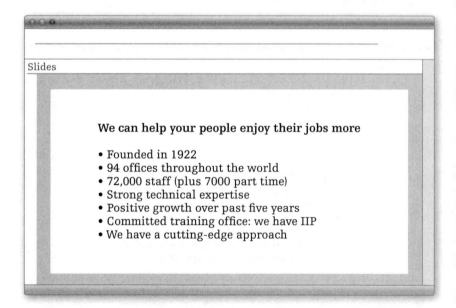

Slides

We can help your people enjoy their jobs more

- Founded in 1922
- 94 offices throughout the world
- 72,000 staff (plus 7000 part time)
- Strong technical expertise
- Positive growth over past five years
- Committed training office: we have IIP
- We have a cutting-edge approach

This doesn't take long, but makes a big difference. Admittedly, it still looks horrible – the next steps will remedy this – but at least it's now in the audience's interest to hear it.

Incidentally, if you don't know why they'll find the slide interesting, they won't!

STEP 2: PRIORITIZE YOUR POINTS

People remember more of your top points than the bottom. It's the same with paragraphs – you remember the top line more than the last. So the second step is to re-order your points, with the best (from the audience's point of view) at the top and the worst at the bottom:

> **We can help your people enjoy their jobs more**
>
> - Strong technical expertise
> - Committed training office: we have IIP
> - We have a cutting-edge approach
> - 94 offices throughout the world
> - Positive growth over past five years
> - 72,000 staff (plus 7000 part time)
> - Founded in 1922

Again, this takes hardly any time – it's just cut and paste.

STEP 3: REMOVE AS MANY LOW-PRIORITY POINTS AS POSSIBLE

One reason that slides become cluttered is because presenters use them as speaker prompts.

But slides are supposed to help the *audience*, not the presenter. After all, the presenter can put her notes on a table, rather than on the big shiny screen that everyone can see.

So remove your unimportant points. This is extremely easy to do, because you put these at the bottom in Step 2. So, Step 3 is simply to (if possible) remove the bottom point; then second bottom; and so on, until you come to one that's too important to remove.

I like this step:

- It only takes a few seconds
- But it means you've wiped out your worst bits
- And it doesn't do any harm – after all, you can still verbalize these points if you want to

Our slide might now show:

Can you see how the first three steps have made this slide much better already? Now let's make it even more impactful.

STEP 4: REMOVE THE UNIMPORTANT WORDS

When presenting, there are two "people" speaking – the presenter and the slides. You don't want both "people" saying exactly the same words (it's boring; and you might as well just hand your slides out for people to read).

This means that, although the presenter speaks in full sentences, your slides shouldn't. Step 4 removes all the non-key words, leaving us with:

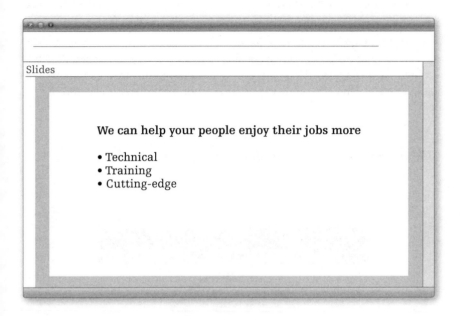

STEP 5: INSERT SLIDE-BUILDS

Please don't think of a green monkey.

I imagine you thought of a green monkey.

Similarly, if you show lots of points on a slide, and ask the audience not to read ahead, they'll read ahead.

But you don't want them to. You want them listening to you, not wishing you'd hurry up and get to later points they've already read.

The only way to stop an audience reading ahead is to click to bring up the next point. In our example, this would mean three clicks for the three points. (By the way, it's better if each point just appears. Having it whoosh in from the left, or do a sweeping arc from the right, is just distracting and annoying.)

STEP 6: MAKE THE SLIDES LOOK NICE

You've now got your slide content right. The only problem? It still looks very unappealing. So, we need to change this.

There are hundreds of books on creating good visuals (if you want to read up on this, Nancy Duarte's books, *Slide:ology* and *Resonate* are worth a read). But, even without reading these, there are lots of improvements you can make very quickly. Here are three ideas. None take long, but each dramatically improve the look:

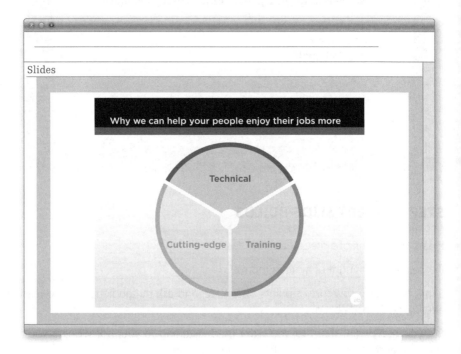

There are other designs, of course, but you get the idea. And every one of these is miles better than where we started:

Even better, of course, the changes took virtually no time to do.

Let's finish with two final tips . . .

USEFUL TIP 1: PREPARE TWO SLIDE-SETS, NOT ONE

You'll use PowerPoint in one of two ways:

1.   As an accompaniment when you're presenting; and/or
2.   To send before/after/instead of your presentation, as a permanent record

These two uses pose a problem regarding what to put on your slides:

- The former needs *sparse* slides, prepared using the six steps in this chapter.
- The latter needs *full* slides (since you're not there, the slides must contain *everything*).

Therefore, it's *impossible* for one slide-set to satisfy both objectives. How can something only tell part of a story, whilst simultaneously telling the entire story?

So, when you're presenting alongside – and also emailing separately – a slide-set, prepare two versions: one sparse and one full.

This sounds like twice the work. But it isn't. You just create the full set, then create a duplicate set using the six Slide Rules.

Since the two slide-sets now give both audience types everything they need, both types of presentation are more likely to work first time. So, weird though it sounds, it's much quicker to create two versions, not one.

USEFUL TIP 2: PREPARING "COMPARE AND CONTRAST" SLIDES

Let's now look at how to apply the six steps to an important topic that people rarely do well – showing how your proposed idea is better than the alternatives. For instance, when persuading:

- Bosses to accept your proposal.
- Your team to change behaviours.
- Customers to choose you over the competition.
- Before and after comparisons, to show the "after" is much better.

You do this using what I call "Plumber Slides". Imagine you have a burst water pipe and ask a plumber if they can help you. The plumber replies by explaining how great their process is, using this slide:

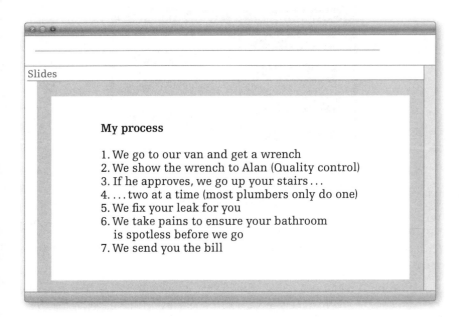

Well, it's not great, is it? As before, you'll probably think "This is *terrible*. It's boring. It isn't tailored to me. I just don't care".

You're also probably thinking "Hurry up – my house is flooding".

There are two main problems with this slide:

- It doesn't address your audience's key issue – the sodden carpets; and
- Your audience can't compare and contrast. Is this process better/worse/the same as other plumbers?

You address the first of these by improving the title; and the second by drawing out the differences (all plumbers do points 1, 3, 5 and 7, but only this one does 2, 4 and 6).

So, a better slide – having applied the slide rules – would be:

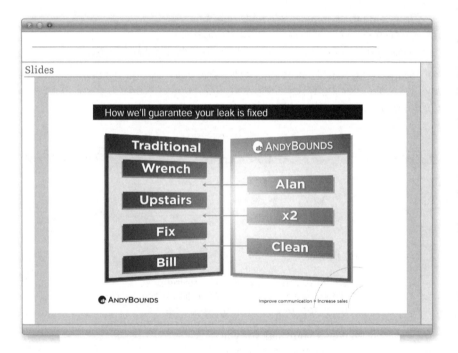

You'd click to show each of the three right-hand side points separately, to allow for discussion.

Look how much better this is than the original. It's nicer to look at. It shows why this plumber's better than the alternatives. It's benefits-rich. It's easier to follow . . . it's just more *persuasive*. And remember: it's the *same* plumber.

You can transform your messages – and therefore your enjoyment of delivering them – by transforming your slides. Your visuals are that important. What changes would your audiences *love* you to make?

Build Your Snowball: Create Great Visuals to Enhance Your Message

Follow my six Slide Rules:

Step 1: Improve your title by including something that interests/
           benefits your audience.
Step 2: Prioritize your points – main ones at the top; worst at
           the bottom.
Step 3: Remove as many "worst" points as possible.
Step 4: Remove the unimportant words.
Step 5: Insert slide-builds so your audience doesn't read ahead.
Step 6: Design the slides so they impress.

And, when you're showing your proposal is better than the alternative, use the Plumber Slide (the second one, not the first.)

40

When you want to start a presentation brilliantly (when your audience is large and/or doesn't know you)

Have you ever looked at a conference speaker and thought "Why am I listening to *you*?"

That's pretty unpleasant for you.

And it's *terrible* for him.

Similarly, when *you're* the speaker, you want your audience to think – before you even walk on stage:

1. I need to hear this topic; and
2. From this person.

To help achieve both, ask your introducer to say two things:

1. Why your topic is critical to the audience; and
2. Why you can help.

For example:

> "As we all know, things are difficult right now. Our competitors continue to raise their game. Our customers are demanding more and more from us, for no extra money. We have to go up a level.
>
> I'm delighted to say that our next speaker will help us do that. She's an acknowledged expert on transformational change. Her book X is the reference book in this area. Her client X said 'XXX' about her. Ladies and gentlemen, please welcome on stage Mrs X."

Without the first paragraph, the audience might think "Why am I listening?"; without the second, "Why am I listening to *her*?"

And, of course, it's much better for *someone else* – not you – to say how great you are (even if you've written the intro for them – something your introducer will often ask you to do anyway).

START WITH A BANG

So, your intro couldn't have gone better. But there's now the small matter of delivering a high-impact Sentence One. And, even after a great introduction, it's not easy to hook them instantly. So, try this:

1. Before your presentation, ask around to find your audience's 2–3 biggest concerns.
2. Start your presentation with the phrase "Have you ever", followed by these concerns.

For example, I recently spoke at a conference where I discovered the audience felt their jobs were ruined by needless conference calls, meetings and presentations. So I started my keynote with:

> *Good morning everyone. I have some questions for you:*
>
> *Have you ever been on a conference call that was terrible? [audience laughter and murmurs of agreement]*
>
> *Have you ever attended a meeting and thought "Why am I here?" [More laughter and agreement]*
>
> *Have you ever been to a presentation and thought: "Please give me a print-out of your slides and let me go. I can read them much quicker than you're going to." [More laughter and agreement]*

After just four sentences, they were thinking "This guy understands me. He's done his research" and – more importantly – "He can help me. He's worth listening to."

So, introducing presentations with "Have you ever" can be very useful. Did you notice how this chapter started?

 Build Your Snowball: Start A Presentation Brilliantly

When your audience doesn't know you, ask your introducer to say:

- Why your topic is critical to this audience ("Our sales have gone down").
- Why you and your expertise will help ("This is why we've invited Britain's Sales Trainer of the Year to help us").

Then, when you start, one technique for creating a powerful first sentence is to say "Have you ever", followed by their biggest concerns ("Have you ever spoken to a customer who looks like they're going to buy... And then they just *don't*?").

That way, in just three sentences – two from the introducer and one from you – your audience is hooked, so you can go about your business of helping them.

41

When you want to appear polished, even if you haven't practised much

You often have two conflicting issues when presenting:

- You want to look polished and impressive.
- This takes time to achieve, and you haven't got much of it.

This chapter addresses both. In fact, my customers frequently tell me this chapter's technique – called "bye-hi" – has the highest value:time ratio, in that it:

1. Brings lots of value.
2. Takes minimal time.
3. Is much better than the more commonly used alternatives:
   Doing lots of full run-throughs. This tends to mean you spend less time on the ending than the beginning, so the presentation often fizzles out. Also it doesn't flow that well.
   Writing the script in full. This makes presenters too robotic and not focused enough on the audience.
   Winging it on the day. Unless you're very skilled and/or lucky, this is unlikely to be as good as if you'd practiced (and, even if it does go well, imagine what you could have achieved if you'd rehearsed).

Bye-hi works when you're presenting either as part of a team or on your own. I'll start with the former, then show how to apply it to the latter.

POLISHED PRESENTING (WHEN YOU'RE IN A TEAM)

A relay race is often won or lost at the baton change. After all, runners are great at running. It's the handover where problems can arise.

Similarly, presenting teams often come unstuck at the "speaker change". After all, presenters are great at presenting. It's the handover where problems can arise.

So, just as relay teams repeatedly practice their baton changes, so too must your team practice your handovers.

This is where you use bye-hi: at the end of her slot, Presenter One says "bye" to her subject (because it's finished) and "hi" to Presenter Two's (because it's starting):

> "So (bye) I've shown how this project will help our workforce. But (hi) the financials have to stack up too, something that Jane will now run through with you."

A bye-hi will help your audience know that the topic is changing. They also seamlessly introduce the next presenter, who can crack on with her topic rather than introducing it herself.

POLISHED PRESENTING (WHEN YOU'RE ON YOUR OWN)

Similarly, when you're presenting on your own, use bye-hi to link your topics, slides and messages. This means that the quickest and best way for you to practise is:

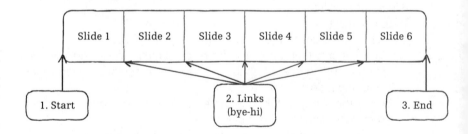

In other words, script, fine-tune and practice your:

1. Start: this *must* be good. If it isn't, the rest might well not be.
2. Links (bye-hi): a good check you've got this right – when you read all your links in order, they should tell the story of your presentation.
3. End: this must also be good, so your audience does what you want them to.

Once your start, links and end are flowing well, do a run-through – quickly at first, to check the flow; then more detailed.

Let's finish with another bye-hi:

So, that's covered the detail behind how to practice quickly. Let's now look at a quick summary of the key points . . .

Build Your Snowball: Appear Polished, Even If You Haven't Practiced Much

The best way to look polished – and the quickest way to practice – is to script and practice your start, links and end (i.e. everything apart from the content). For your links, use bye-hi: say *bye* to the previous topic and *hi* to the next one.

Once these are flowing well, incorporate your content into the next run-through.

42

When you want to prepare for – and deliver – an excellent Q&A session

We've all sat through great presentations which were ruined by a tedious Q&A. It just ends up depressing for everyone.

Since Q&As make or break your presentations, you must be brilliant at them. But, despite their importance, most people don't give them the attention they deserve. Do these pie charts sound like you?

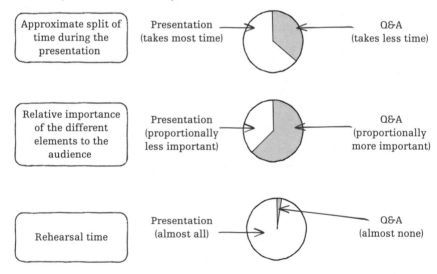

You'll have your own proportions for your situation of course. But, in my experience, it's rare to find people who practice Q&As as much as they should, given how important they are.

Here are nine simple techniques to help you deliver excellent Q&As:

1. Be clear
Tell people upfront whether you want questions during your talk, or at the end (it's often a good idea to check protocol with the organizer beforehand).

2. Be quick
When Mr. X asks a question, it's quite possible only Mr. X cares about the answer. Don't assume the whole audience does. Once you realize you might be boring everybody apart from Mr. X, your answers become much more punchy.

3. Shut up
Once Mr. X is happy with your answer, move on – even if you know more about the topic.

4. Don't overrun
Your audience thinks the Q&A is part of your allotted time. So don't allow it to cause you to overrun. Nobody's ever grateful you did.

If you think you might go over your time, ask them whether they want you to continue or to wrap things up.

5. Start well
Avoid the dreaded tumbleweed moment that often follows "Does anyone have a question?" Instead, use the more positive "So, who has my first question?"

6. Prepare properly
Rehearse answers to likely questions, including the ones you're dreading.

After all, if you don't, you can pretty much guarantee somebody will ask them, and you then need to create your wonderful answer "live" in front of a potentially hostile audience.

7. Remove concerns
If you know your audience is worried about a topic, pre-empt and remove their concerns during your presentation – "I know that many of you are worried about the cost of this. Let me put your minds at rest by showing that . . ."

If you don't, they might ask awkward questions about it.

Or, even worse, they won't – which means they'll leave the room still worried.

8. Easy Peasy

Here's a technique that helps you frame answers to difficult questions. It's one that's often taught on Customer Service courses – ECPC (Easy Peasy):

Empathize – "I can see why you're worried about the impact on your colleagues."

Clarify – "Can I be clear that it's just the inbound calls you're concerned about? Or, does it extend to outbound too?"

Propose – "In that case, I suggest we deal with it as follows . . ."

Confirm – "Does this answer your question?"

9. Never guess

If you don't know the answer to a question, never guess. It's the wrong thing to do. And people see right through it, whatever you think. Plus, you have to remember what you've said – and you probably won't.

Instead, say something like "That's a great question. I don't have all the information to answer it now. I'll speak to Mrs. X this afternoon, and promise to get back to you before the end of the day."

Do all nine, and your Q&As will be more impactful. This means you will be.

Build Your Snowball: Prepare For – and Deliver – An Excellent Q&A Session

Q&As are a critical part of your presentations, so need practicing.

Nine tips to help you handle them well are:

- Be clear whether you want questions throughout or at the end.
- Be quick – satisfy the questioner; don't tell them *everything*.
- Shut up as soon as the questioner is happy.
- Don't overrun on your time.
- Start well – "So, who has my first question?" will get a question.
- Prepare properly – be ready for all likely questions, especially the horrible ones.
- Remove concerns – avoid them asking about an awkward topic by mentioning it in your talk.
- Easy Peasy – **E**mpathize, **C**larify, **P**ropose, **C**onfirm.
- Never guess – if you don't know, say you'll find out.

43

When you want to ensure your important initiatives succeed

Have you ever tried to launch a new initiative, but it didn't go well?

That's just a horrible situation, and one you won't want to repeat.

Two techniques that will help future launches go better are:

1. **Communicating upfront:** discover – as early as possible – your key people's goals, hopes and concerns with your initiative. Then adapt your approach and communications to show how your initiative addresses these areas.
2. **Communicate throughout:** keep talking – communicate proactively and effectively before, during and after your initiative.

STEP 1: COMMUNICATING UPFRONT

One of my customers was recently about to launch a new initiative, which included recruiting a new senior team. They wanted to explain to their workforce how things would work, and the benefits these new recruits would bring to the company.

I advised that they ask questions beforehand, to make sure their communications focused on the right things. When they did this, they discovered people weren't excited at all. In fact, they were fearful for their jobs. They thought these new "superstars" would mean redundancy or demotion.

Once we knew this, our communications changed in every way. They had to. But, can you imagine the disaster that would have happened if we hadn't asked?

So, you *have* to ask upfront, to find their goals, hopes and concerns. Incidentally, good questions are: What are your goals? Your hopes? Your concerns?

If there aren't many people, ask them individually or in small groups. If there are lots, it might be quickest to survey them. There's lots of good survey software around – much of it cheap – so it's easy to do. It's also easy to get it wrong, so remember:

You want the survey to...	To achieve this...
Be easy for them to start	Ask simple, closed questions early on (a bonus of closed questions: it's much easier and quicker for you to summarize responses).
Be easy and quick to complete	Ask as few questions as possible.
Show clear benefits of completing the survey	Put something engaging in the survey's title and/or your covering email.
Give a balanced view	Ask for both their positive and negative thoughts about your initiative.
Be clear how long it will take to complete	Tell them.
Be completed promptly	Give them a deadline.
Be clear what happens next	Tell them what you'll do with their responses.

Here's an example of how your covering email might therefore look:

Let's stop wasting time doing needless things

All of us are too busy. We need to free up some time.

As a management team, we're committed to changing our working practices, to give you the time you need to do the job you want to do.

To help us focus on the right areas, please can you click on the link below and answer a few quick questions about your priorities? It will only take two minutes max.

We'll then incorporate your views into our changes. We'll also share a summary of everyone's responses with you.

We want to move quickly with this, so the deadline for your responses is INSERT DATE. The link to the survey is INSERT LINK.

We're asking everyone for their views on this. So, please do respond by the deadline so we can include yours.

Thanks for your help.

The link again: INSERT LINK

STEP 2: COMMUNICATING THROUGHOUT

Once you know everyone's goals, hopes and concerns, plan your communication approach accordingly. This is much better than the frequently-seen-but-never-good "Right, I've now finished my initiative. Who shall I tell?"

Clearly, the earlier you consider your communication, the better – and shorter – it's going to be. Also, preparing early allows you to proactively build anticipation by saying such things as:

- "Our initiative's uncovered some useful insights already. I was assuming I'd share these later, but would you prefer a quick update now?"
- "I'm looking forward to discussing our findings. I can already see there'll be huge cost savings for us."

And here's some proof that "early is good":

I've worked with many companies to help important initiatives land. Many of them first approached me towards the end of the initiative, when they had a *problem*.

Almost always, they hadn't prepared early enough: they hadn't asked questions upfront and/or hadn't considered the communication element at all.

Interestingly, they now call me at the *start* of key projects not the end. This ensures they do the right preparation at the right time. Understandably, this has made a huge difference to how well their initiatives land.

So, what could you do, to think about your communication earlier than you do now?

Build Your Snowball: Ensure Your Important Initiatives Succeed

Remember the two key steps:

1. Communicate upfront – find people's goals, hopes and concerns about your initiative, so you can tailor your communications accordingly.

2. Communicate throughout – proactively communicate the right messages at the right time. Don't leave it till the end before you do it/ think about it.

44

When you want to have good two-way conversations

Have you noticed how some people don't have good conversations? Instead, they take turns to monologue:

Alice: I had a good meeting today. Sally signed off my project.
Bob: I did too. We had the most effective Board meeting we've ever had.
Alice: I know what you mean. I was dreading asking Sally. You know what she's like.
Bob: I know. And our Board meetings always drag on.

At first glance, it looks like Alice and Bob are chatting. They're not. They're discussing *totally different things*.

When we chat, we should – as Dr Stephen Covey said "seek first to understand, then to be understood". A better approach would be:

Alice: I had a good meeting today. Sally signed off my project.
Bob: Great – tell me what happened.
Alice: I was dreading asking her. You know what she's like.
Bob: I know. So, how did you convince her?
Alice: Well, I . . . [tells story].
Bob: And how did you feel?
Alice: To be honest, relieved. I . . . [tells story].
Bob: Well done. I had a good meeting today too.

This version is much better. Bob listened to Alice. He responded to what she said, rather than waiting for his turn to speak. She, in turn, is now more likely to show interest in his topic. After all, when both parties listen, both parties benefit.

Which of the two conversations sounds like you? If it can be the former, the good news is that this is one of those important areas that's quite easy to fix, in that you "just" have to do three things:

1. Talk less: if you're talking, you're not listening. So, when you think it's your turn to speak, remember to WAIT, which stands for **W**hy **A**m **I T**alking?

2. Ask more: when someone says something, rather than giving your point of view, ask questions to uncover more.

3. Remember to do it: this is the hardest – partly because the first two aren't hard, but mainly because it's hard to remember *when it matters* in a conversation. To help with this, you can:

   when talking on the phone, write "Ask" or "WAIT" in big letters on your notepad; and/or

   insert a weekly diary reminder called "Which meetings shall I ask more/talk less in this week?"

And, of course, you can tell when it *isn't* working, because a conversation won't be going as planned.

When this happens, simply ask yourself "Am I talking too much/asking too little?" If so, start asking the other person to explain what they've just said, to give more detail etc. You'll find the benefits of doing so far outweigh the problems if you don't.

Build Your Snowball: Have Good Two-Way Conversations

You want to dialogue, not swap monologues. So, focus intently on their words. Ask them to expand on what they've just said, to give examples... *anything* that ensures you're both focusing on the same thing.

And, when you think it's your turn to speak, remember to **WAIT** – **W**hy **A**m **I T**alking?

45

When you want to enjoy attending networking events

"Working a room" is an important business skill. But it isn't easy. How to start? What to say? How to make it an interesting two-way conversation? And – something people often ask for help with – how to get away from someone boring, without being rude!

Most people don't feel comfortable networking. In fact, I've found that many think it's harder for them than others. For instance, I recently asked a conference audience of 450-ish whether they thought networking was harder for them than everybody else in the room. Virtually everybody put their hands up. I said "Well, you can't *all* be right!"

Yes, networking is hard. But it's hard for pretty much everybody. This chapter removes all that, by showing you the four steps of a successful networking conversation.

But, before that, here are some simple guidelines to help you enjoy networking, rather than just "get through it":

- Remember: the aim of networking is to find useful people, and agree to meet them again at a later date. This means that working a room is "only" a:
  - filtering exercise: will it benefit you both if you see them again?
  - diary exercise: if you *do* want to meet, agree when you'll do so.
- Be polite. Ask about them first. Listen intently. Don't rant on about yourself. Don't look over their shoulder as they're talking, trying to find someone "more interesting".

- Networking is *not* selling. Nobody will make a buying decision at a networking event (even if they seem mad keen, you'll still have to meet later to do the paperwork). So, just aim for a subsequent meeting, not a sale.
- Make sure you're in the right room. If you want to speak to CEOs, go to rooms full of CEOs. Also, whenever possible, look at the Guest List beforehand, to identify who you want to meet.
- You only need two things at a networking event: business cards and a pen. If you forget one of these, let it be your business cards – you absolutely need a pen, as you'll see below. After all, you can always use their card to contact them.

THE FOUR STEPS OF A PLEASANT, PRODUCTIVE NETWORKING CONVERSATION

1. In	2. You	3. Me	4. Out

Step 1: In
Get *into* the conversation. Approach someone and ask "Can I join you?"

When they say "yes" (and they will – who'd be so rude as to blurt out "NO"?), you've completed this step already.

Step 2: You
Talk about them first. It's easier, since you don't have to think of amazing things to say about yourself. It's more polite. It helps them feel comfortable with you – after all, people love talking about themselves. And, because you're learning about them, you can tailor what you say about yourself later on.

To get them talking, ask good questions. There are three main types:

Question type	Examples	Comments
Introductory	What do you do? How's business?	They're useful, but unlikely to unearth valuable insights. So, be brief.
Unearthing	In your company, what are you responsible for? What have you been brought in to achieve? What are your goals this year?	Asking about their *future* uncovers where they want to get to. This helps you understand their priorities, so you can position yourself as someone who can help them – either yourself, or by introducing them to someone who can.
The Big Question	Who are good contacts for you?	This is useful to know if you're to help them. It's also a great tool to get *out* of the conversation, as you'll see later.

> **To make this step easy: prepare a list of questions and discussion topics, so you're not searching for them in the middle of a conversation.**

Step 3: Me

They will then ask about you. Remember, it's more interesting to talk about the AFTERs you *cause* – "I help companies pay less tax" – than what you *do* – "I'm an accountant" (chapter 31 has more detail on how to craft enticing Elevator Pitches).

When they ask for more information, remember "Facts Tell Stories Sell". It's more interesting, memorable and compelling for them to hear successes you've helped others achieve than it is to hear about your products and services (and *please* don't whip out your brochure).

> **To make this step easy: prepare your Elevator Pitch and 2–3 relevant success stories in advance.**

Step 4: Out

At the end of your conversation, if you want to follow-up afterwards, ask their permission:

- *Ask* for their business card.
- *Ask* when they want you to call them.
- *Ask* if you can write this date/time on the back of their card (this makes it "official" that you'll be calling).

Then, end the conversation with "I've enjoyed talking to you tonight. I'll call you on Monday, as agreed" (Note the past tense here – "*I enjoyed*": this shows the conversation is over).

If you *don't* want to follow-up, use their answer to step 2's Big Question:

"I've enjoyed our conversation. You mentioned earlier that you want to speak to surveyors. If I bump into any, would you like me to pass them your way?" [Yes please] "Great, I will do. Enjoy your evening."

To make this step easy: prepare and practice your closing lines.

THE MOST IMPORTANT THING ABOUT NETWORKING

The crux of networking is that you *must* follow-up. If you don't, everything in this chapter becomes a waste of time. So, call when you said you would; prepare what you said you would; help as you said you would; and if your follow-up is *written*, make sure it impresses (the next chapter has more on this).

Having the ability and discipline to follow-up sets you apart. Far too many people don't (I imagine you could name a few, without thinking too hard). But it's an effective, quick way to build quality relationships with quality people.

Build Your Snowball: Enjoy Attending Networking Events

Networking's *only* purpose is to filter out who you want to speak with after the event, and arrange a time when you'll do so.

You'll do this well – and quickly – if you think in/you/me/out:

- In – get into the conversation quickly.
- You – ask good questions to find out about the other person.
- Me – talk about what you *cause* (not do), using stories to add interest/credibility.
- Out – get out of the conversation politely, ensuring there's a positive next step.

46

When you want to help people read your documents quickly

Writing documents is rarely fun.

And then pity the poor person who has to read them. Even if you've done a great job, your reader will be busy, have competing priorities, and want to see your key points as quickly as possible. Sad to say, your document might not (won't?) be their Number 1 Priority that day.

Since very few people love reading documents – and *nobody* likes reading them twice – readers need to glean your key points quickly. And, since you're spending X hours creating it, you might as well spend Y minutes making it easy to read.

There have been many studies into what people find easiest to read. None of them are very surprising, but it's always good to be reminded of these things:

Readers prefer...	Because...
Portrait, not landscape	People's eyes prefer reading narrower columns, rather than sweeping across wide ones. That's why newspaper columns are so narrow – it helps us read them quickly.
Short paragraphs – maximum four lines	Longer paragraphs cause people to lose concentration and retention.
Short sentences	It's simpler to make out all your points when they're in separate sentences. A common mistake is to make a sentence too long by joining two sentences with "and" or "but".
Lots of white space	It's easier on the eye; and it breaks things into manageable chunks.
Minimal use of capitals	Research shows people find it easier to read lower case. AND CAPITALS LOOK LIKE YOU'RE SHOUTING.
Lots of relevant sub-headings	When people skim-read, they often read headings and the top 1–2 lines of paragraphs. So: Include more headings – at least one per page. Since you've now shortened your paragraphs, there'll be more "top 1–2 lines".
Good graphics	Everyone knows good visuals help.
Congruent look and feel	If your message is important, your document must look like it is too.

As I say, this table contains few surprises. I guess the biggest surprise is that people often don't do all of them.

Do you do all these well? To check, look at a couple of your recent documents. Could you make 1–2 simple improvements, to make things easier for the reader?

Build Your Snowball: Help People Read Your Documents Quickly

Lay out your documents so people can see your main points quickly:

- Portrait, not landscape.
- Short paragraphs.
- Short sentences.
- Lots of white space.
- Minimal use of capitals.
- Lots of relevant sub-headings.
- Good graphics.
- Congruent look and feel.

47

When you want to improve people's performance through observation and coaching

"Are our lawyers good on the phone?"

One of my legal customers asked me this the other day. He wanted to know how customer focused his people are. So, I called six firms, including his, telling each of them I'd been in a car crash and asking whether they could help me.

Every one of them asked great Lawyer Questions: "Where did it happen?", "Were there any witnesses?", "Have you called the police?" And so on.

But do you know what *not one* of them asked?

"Are you OK?"

They were so focused on following the process that they forgot the #1 output: to make sure the customer was alright.

I thought that was pretty alarming. Even worse, if their manager had been observing them, he could well have said they'd done well, because they'd ticked all the steps on their Observation Forms. This shows the problems with these forms – they're often:

- Process focused ("Did you follow the steps?"), rather than output-focused ("Did it work?"); and/or
- Too long.

If this sounds like your company, your observations won't improve things sufficiently. After all, since people **RE**spect what you **IN**spect, your forms should focus on your high-priority outputs only. For example, let's say your colleagues'

presentations are too long, too boring and never achieve the desired result. In this case, your observations might only need cover:

Observation sheet: improving presentations	
Before	**After**
What did you want your audience to do after your presentation?	Did they?
Did the *audience* enjoy it?	What would have helped *them* enjoy it more?
Did *you* enjoy it?	What would have helped *you* enjoy it more?
What one improvement will you make next time?	

Or, if you currently observe whether your salespeople follow each step of the sales process (1. Did you build rapport? 2. Did you ask good open questions? and so on), better questions might be:

Observation sheet: increasing sales	
Before	**After**
What did you think the customer's greatest benefit of the meeting would be?	Was it?
What did you want the customer to do after the meeting?	Did they?
What one improvement will you make next time?	

Both examples are very similar to ones I've used on countless occasions. Each time, they've helped transform behaviours, because they're focusing on only a few (not many) outputs (not inputs).

Also, did you notice how both ended with:

"What one improvement will you make next time?"

As you know, people need something to work on, or they won't work on anything. And, it's important to give them something manageable, because of how busy they are. Improving their performance by one thing each time will often provide much better results than giving them 15 areas to focus on after every observation.

Let's end with a quick question: What one improvement will *you* make to your observations next time?

Build Your Snowball: Improve People's Performance through Observation and Coaching

Make sure your observations focus on:

- A few things only, not too many.
- Outputs not inputs ("Did it work?" not "Did you follow all the steps?").
- Resulting actions – there *must* be 1–2 actionable next steps.

To build momentum, start Observation Two by referencing Observation One's next steps.

48

When you want to improve people's performance after annual reviews

Every year, my children show their school reports to their proud father. Like most reports, they focus almost entirely on how they've done during the past year, with a couple of comments about how to improve next year.

A lot of staff appraisals are like that: lots about last year and less about next. These serve a purpose, but often can be too retrospective and "discussing", rather than future-focused and "directing".

HOLD PREVIEWS, NOT REVIEWS

There are lots of reasons for reviews having this past-focus. One is the title. Calling them "Reviews" leads people to *review* past performance, much like a school report.

My company – and many of my customers – never have performance *reviews*. Instead, we add a "P" to the title and have *Previews*, often accompanied by a benefits-rich subtitle "Ensuring you have a great next year".

This changes everyone's focus entirely. And although our previews contain some past-based discussions – we mustn't ignore last year, after all – the overwhelming focus is on how we can make things even better next year.

Self-test 1 – Review and Preview

During your staff reviews, what's the split between discussing the past compared to the future? 50:50? 90:10? 10:90?

Does this split feel appropriate? Or would you both benefit from being more future-focused?

What change(s) could you make to improve this?

FOCUS ON THE "WHAT AND HOW", NOT JUST THE "WHAT"

Imagine a sales team of two people. One smashes targets all the time, but is horrible to work with; the other sometimes hits targets, but embodies your company's values and is a joy to work with. Which do you value most?

This isn't an easy question, and there's no "right" answer. But to deliver great (p) reviews, you need to:

- Know which is more important to you.
- Ensure your (p)review materials support this. For instance, I've seen companies say "The customer is king", but their review forms focus almost entirely on whether staff hit their sales numbers for different product lines.

Self-test 2 – What and How

During staff reviews, what's the split of discussing *what* people do, compared with *how* they do it? 50:50? 90:10? 10:90?

Does this split feel appropriate?

What change(s) could you make to improve this?

GET THE FOUNDATIONS RIGHT

(P)reviews are like buildings: the foundations are essential. And although nobody would ever say "Hmmm, *nice* foundations", you'd sure miss them if they weren't there.

Self-test 3 – The Foundations

Do you always do all of these?

1. Arrive on time to the review, with a clear diary.
2. Give them 100% of your focus, and not be distracted by outside issues.
3. Allow them to overrun if needed.
4. Use a suitable venue.
5. Keep the date sacred (never bumping it for something "more important").
6. Ensure total confidentiality.
7. Complete your pre-work.
8. Ensure that, in the meeting, they speak at least as much as you do.
9. Recognize successes.
10. Proactively manage underperformance.
11. Work so closely with them throughout the year that the meeting contains no surprises.
12. Make sure you both have actions at the end.
13. Do your follow-ups on time.
14. Manage your team properly during the year, not just for a one-hour (p)review.
15. Think the meetings are worthwhile.
16. Ensure your colleagues think they're worthwhile.

School reports are useful. Parents Evenings that discuss "next year" are even better.

Staff reviews are useful. Previews are even better.

Which do you do? And, what change(s) would improve this?

Build Your Snowball: Improve People's Performance after Annual Reviews

Reviews improve performance when you:

- Focus on the future, not just the past (**P**review, not review).
- Focus on behaviours, not just actions (the What *and* the How).
- Get the foundations right (arrive on time, never postpone it for "something more important", no interruptions and so on).

49

When you want to improve people's performance when you delegate to them

"If I'd asked my customers what they wanted, they'd have said a faster horse."
Henry Ford

I love this quote. It makes me smile. And it also makes a great point:

> As long as the expert (Henry Ford) knows the beneficiary's (customer's) desired *future* (to go faster), then the expert can apply his skills to help achieve it.

In fact, the *expert* is bound to know more about how they can help than the beneficiary ever could, because they're the *expert*. This is one of the reasons Steve Jobs didn't believe in customer research, saying that it was Apple's job to know what customers wanted before they did.

This concept has big implications when you're delegating (in other words, when you're the *beneficiary*).

When buying from suppliers:

- Don't specify the deliverables ("Please give me a new computer system").
- Instead, explain your desired *future*, and ask how they can best help ("We want our office to be more efficient, removing our bottlenecks and freeing up everyone's time. What do you suggest?").

When delegating to an expert:

- Don't specify how the job is to be done ("I need a report by Friday"). Even if you say "Pretty please, could I possibly have the report by Friday", you're still focusing on the job. As my wife Emma says: "This is like someone barking out orders with fluff on". This stifles people's expertise and/or engagement. It often leads to suboptimal results.
- Instead, explain your desired *future*, and ask the expert how they can best help ("We need to work more closely with the Finance Department. I'd like to have made some progress on this by the end of the week. How do you think we can achieve this?").

Delegating obviously depends on a person's level of expertise. Someone with no experience might need you to guide them on the deliverable. If it helps, brief them using the following approach (it works well in writing or when you talk it through):

My objectives

I want . . . [INSERT YOUR OBJECTIVE I.E. YOUR DESIRED FUTURE STATE]

I know we're not achieving this now because . . . [INSERT YOUR EVIDENCE THERE'S A PROBLEM]

I'll know it's happening when . . . [INSERT YOUR MEASURES OF SUCCESS]

But please bear in mind

We're constrained by [INSERT THE FACTORS THAT MIGHT GET IN THE WAY]

Immediate next steps

Please can you [INSERT ACTION] by [INSERT DEADLINE].

Here's an example of how it might look:

My objectives

I want our colleagues to be more engaged.

I know we're not achieving this now because the Employee Engagement scores are so low. Also, people are turning up later to meetings, and not doing things unless I shout at them!

I'll know it's happening when:

- They turn up to meetings on time.
- They do things I ask first time.
- Our staff survey will show improved Employee Engagement scores.

But please bear in mind

We're constrained by the fact we've another big project this month, so everyone is time-poor. Also, the absolute maximum budget for this is $25,000.

Immediate next steps

Please advise how you think we should progress before the end of the week.

The template makes it crystal clear what you want them to help you achieve, but empowers them to devise the best way to do it. You'll therefore find it often leads to people doing better work in a better way, in a better frame of mind. When you don't do this, even though you don't know it, you might be asking for a faster horse . . .

Build Your Snowball: Improve People's Performance When You Delegate To Them

Delegating *tasks* leads to people doing *tasks*.

But explaining your desired *future* empowers people to use their creativity to help you achieve it. This increases their buy-in, engagement and therefore your likelihood of success. In other words, explain what you want them to *cause*, not do.

SECTION E

Eliminate the negatives

How to remove your communication frustrations

Chapter	When you want to...
50	stop saying "no" too quickly
51	say "no" in a way that doesn't cause you problems
52	come up with good ideas, but can't think of any
53	remove someone's concerns about what you're planning to do
54	remove someone's final reason for saying "no"
55	get good outcomes from challenging conversations
56	stop procrastinating about initiating challenging conversations
57	stop your messages becoming diluted
58	stop diluting other people's messages
59	stop hating presentations
60	avoid people instantly doubting your credibility

Chapter	When you want to ...
61	stop wasting your time with people who can't make decisions
62	prevent avoidable disasters
63	stop saying irrelevant stuff
64	break the pattern of hearing useful ideas, but doing nothing with them

WHY THIS MATTERS

When communication works well, it's great. People are inspired, motivated and happy. Their minds are uncluttered. They focus on the right things. Stuff gets done.

Unfortunately, it often isn't like this. There are the obvious day-to-day issues – too much information, everything's "TOP PRIORITY" and "URGENT", you daren't use the restroom for fear of the number of emails you'll return to.

And there are the less obvious – but equally painful – problems, like how to:

- Say "no" when you know it will cause you problems.
- Remove people's concerns about what you're planning to do.
- Start a conversation you know will be challenging.
- Get a good outcome following a difficult conversation.

When you think about it, communication "only" has to keep both parties happy, achieve the desired outcomes and be as quick as possible. It shouldn't be that hard. But it can be. So, here's how to overcome the communication frustrations you face every day.

50

When you want to stop saying "no" too quickly

The hardest person to convince is often yourself.

After all, you can tell yourself "no" more quickly than anybody else ever could.

There's one simple change you can make to help get past your biggest critic, and help persuade yourself to say "yes" not "no".

Harrison (Buzz) Price carried out the feasibility studies that helped Disney choose the locations of its first few theme parks. He said that, when responding to one of Walt Disney's ideas, you had to say "Yes if", not "No because". You can see why. Imagine if Disney had said "no because" to:

- Can we marry up hand-drawn animation and sound?
- Can we use colour, not black and white?
- Can we make the first ever full-length animated film?
- Can we build a high-quality theme park?
- Can we sell merchandise?

Here's a quick exercise. Answer these six questions as quickly as you can – the only rule is that your first two words are "No because":

Can you apply for a better position/job?
   No because . . .
Can you ask for more pay?
   No because . . .
Can you spend time thinking of a great new idea, and share it with your boss?
   No because . . .
Can you stop holding your weekly team meetings that achieve nothing significant?
   No because . . .
Can you praise people more often than you do?
   No because . . .
Can you take up a new hobby?
   No because . . .

"Yes if" helps you find ways to achieve things that you initially think *can't* be done. So, now, repeat the exercise. This time, the only rule is that your first two words are "Yes if":

Can you apply for a better position/job?
   Yes if . . .
Can you ask for more pay?
   Yes if . . .
Can you spend time thinking of a great new idea, and share it with your boss?
   Yes if . . .
Can you stop holding your weekly team meetings that achieve nothing significant?
   Yes if . . .
Can you praise people more often than you do?
   Yes if . . .
Can you take up a new hobby?
   Yes if . . .

You can see how useful "yes" is when you aren't sure why you're saying "no" (the next chapter shows how to say "no" when you *know* you want to).

In one way, you've only changed two words. But in another way, you've changed *everything*. After all, it can be hard to convince others. But it's *impossible* if you can't first convince yourself.

And now, I have two final questions for you:

Can you think "Yes if" every time it's relevant?
    Yes if . . .
And can you help the people who are critical to your success – your team, boss, customers, suppliers and so on – ensure they think "Yes if" too?
    Yes if . . .

Build Your Snowball: Stop Saying "No" Too Quickly

To overcome your reticence about a good idea, think "Yes if", not "No because". This helps you say "yes" to things that you might have mistakenly turned down too quickly.

51

When you want to say "no" in a way that doesn't cause you problems

We all get asked to do things that we don't want to do.

And it's not always easy to know how to respond. You don't want to appear unhelpful. But it seems you only have two options, neither of which is very good:

1. Say "yes" and wish you hadn't – bad for you and possibly them.
2. Say "no" – bad for them and probably you.

But you have another option:

3. Say "I *can* help you, but not in the way you suggested".

This is often the best option, for both you and them. They get the outcome they wanted; and you've helped them do so. Even better, this approach is relatively straightforward, in that you only have to remember two things:

1. Show willingness to help.
2. Explain that you saying "no" to their original request is in their interest.

Here are some examples:

When you're asked to do something, but are short of time

Them: Can you send me a report on X by Friday?

You: *I can definitely get something to you by then. Exactly what information do you want?*

Them: [Their answer]

You: *Sure, I can do that. With deadlines being so tight, rather than you having to read a full report, I'll do the research and call you Wednesday to discuss it. I can then send over a brief summary of the key points on Thursday. OK?*

When you're asked to do something, but don't feel able to

Them: Can you run a workshop on X for me?

You: *I want to help, but don't think that's the best way I can. I haven't much experience in running workshops like this, and don't want to dilute the work you're doing. Instead, I'll speak to Mark – he's a great facilitator – and brief him on what we need him to cover. I can make sure the workshop works by doing X as well. OK?*

When you're asked to prepare a document which will take you ages, which you doubt will be read

Them: Please send a document through to me next week

You: *I'll be pleased to. I don't want to waste your time giving you information you don't want. So, let me ask a couple of quick questions, so I focus on the right things for you.*

But what about when someone needs your help, and you just haven't any time at all?

This is the hardest one, because you can't do anything about it, even if you wanted to.

You could say something like, "I'd love to help, but I'm back to back – sorry. I hope it goes well for you". This sounds nice enough, but in effect you're just saying "no" beautifully. So they don't benefit from your help, and you don't benefit from helping.

Instead, you have lots of alternatives:

- Recommend someone else who can help – a colleague or supplier you've used before.
- Spend five minutes (let's face it, you can always find five minutes) giving an overview of how they should approach it.
- Give them a similar document you've written before, so they can follow your approach.
- Recommend reading material to help them.
- Ask if their deadline is flexible, so you can help them later.
- Ask your boss/team if anyone has time to help.
- Explain to your boss/team that this has come up, and ask if it should be prioritized over existing work.

Like all the examples in this chapter, the best option can often be something other than a definite "no" (either horrible or beautiful) or a definite "yes". And, once you realize you've lots of choices, it's much easier to say "no" in a way people are happy with.

Build Your Snowball: Say "No" in a Way that Doesn't Cause You Problems

When someone asks you to do something you don't want to, you can respond with "yes", "no" or offer an alternative.

This last option is usually best, especially when they see:

- You're keen to help; and
- Your suggestion suits them better than what they'd proposed.

52

When you want to come up with good ideas, but can't think of any

People aren't good at thinking in threes. For example, you might say to your friend:

Shall we go to the cinema or a restaurant tonight? (two options, not three)
Dinner? OK then – Chinese or Italian?
Italian? OK – Il Forno or San Carlo?

Similarly, as you saw in the previous chapter, when people face challenging situations, they tend to think they have only *two* solutions. And, if neither is satisfactory, they feel powerless to resolve it.

For example, a company recently asked me to help smooth their relationships with some customers. They were worried because, in the face of an onslaught from an irate customer, they felt they'd only had two options – back down or fight – and neither appealed. They wanted to know how to react if it happened again.

I advised they should find the often-elusive *third* option, which would have lots of advantages:

- They'd have 50% more choice – three, not two.
- Because they'd had to think more deeply, they'd find the third option could well be best.
- Once they had the third option, floodgates usually open to give options 4, 5 and 6. So they'd now have *lots* more choice.

When I asked for a third option, they thought for a while, then said "next time, we could take a break from the meeting". And when I prompted with "anything else?", lots more appeared:

- Invite a colleague to join the meeting.
- Say "sorry – can you repeat that?" (complaints don't have the same intensity second time around).
- Break the customer's flow by saying "I'm confused" followed by silence. When they reply "why?", you've regained control.
- Persuasively and empathetically help remove the customer's concerns (see the next chapter for how).
- Apologize.
- Agree.
- Disagree.
- Ask them to slow down, so that you can take notes (this can dampen their "energetic fury").
- Arrange another meeting.
- The second meeting could be at your premises.
- Or theirs.
- Or a neutral venue.
- Or on the phone.
- And so on . . .

When they thought they had two options – and neither worked – they felt there was nothing they could do.

Once they realized they had *lots* of options, they knew they could influence the situation.

And, once you've convinced yourself, you've a much better chance of convincing someone else.

So, here's a quick exercise: Think of a current problem you have. Quickly identify two actions you could take to resolve it:

1. _____

2. _____

And now come up with a third:

3. _____

Let's see if you can open the floodgates:

4. _____

5. _____

6. _____

7. _____

Now you have lots more options, choose the one(s) most likely to work.

So, as a general rule, when you think you have no options, assume you have at least three. It's just a case of finding them. In fact, "thinking in threes" is a useful technique to embed. It helps you see options others can't, and more quickly.

So, what can you do, to ensure "thinking in threes" becomes your default?

Option 1 _____

Option 2 _____

Option 3 _____

Build Your Snowball: Come Up With Good Ideas

When you want to make better decisions, think in threes, not twos. The more you uncover third options – something people don't often do – the more chance you have of finding a better way to achieve things.

53

When you want to remove someone's concerns about what you're planning to do

I was held up at airport security last week, by one of the sweetest things I've ever seen.

A small girl in front of me – I guess she was four or five – was devastated that someone wanted to take her Disney Princess Bag from her. She was distraught: tears, screaming . . . the works.

Her parents reassured her that the bag was just being x-rayed and she'd get it back immediately. But she wasn't buying that. Life had lost all meaning if someone took her bag from her.

After a couple of minutes (I'm sure it felt longer to them), Modern Parenting was replaced by Victorian Parenting, and her Dad snatched the bag and whisked it through security. The girl got the bag back 10 seconds later, but I doubt her vocal cords – or my ears – will ever recover.

You see, sometimes people are concerned about things that don't worry you. Unlike this girl, they won't burst into tears about it, but they *will* say things like "it's too expensive", "we have other priorities", "I'm not sure you're experienced enough", "we've no time", "there's no resource". Even though you might not agree, if they think it's an issue, it is one.

When people have concerns, you have three options:

1. *They* raise the concern. Just like the girl did about her bag, they might do this in a distressed way. Or at the wrong time. Either way, this puts you on the defensive. Not good.

2. *Neither* of you raises it. This is by far the worst. Imagine you're selling some-thing and your customer thinks it's too expensive – if it goes unsaid, they just won't buy. Again, not good.

3. *You* raise it. Weird though it sounds, this is the best option, because the others bring bigger problems.

To raise, and then remove, people's concerns, there are four steps:

Introduce it	State it	Remove it	Confirm it
"You've told me you're concerned that…" "If I was you, I might be thinking…" "In the past, some people have been concerned about…"	"It's too expensive." "We've got other priorities." And so on…	Use *pre-prepared* responses to remove their concerns (see the notes below).	Check they're comfortable – "OK?"

Note: you have to give a persuasive response to their concern. The alternative – "I know you think it's expensive . . . and it is" – is just not very good! The easiest way to find your best response is to think of a few, and then select the best. For instance, responses to concerns about cost could include:

- We've agreed that this is worth $1 million if it goes well, and will only cost $20,000. That's a Return On Investment of over 50/1. I know it's not easy to find the $20,000, but we *have* to. We need to take advantage of opportunities like this.
- Which other budget can we use to pay for it?
- Who can we ask to sponsor this?
- We currently run 100 events a year, each costing around $10,000. Can't we just do 98, and use the freed-up $20,000 to pay for this?
- Shall we stagger the payment?
- Should I go back to the supplier, and ask them to change the payment terms?
- I can free up $10,000 from my budget. Please could you match this figure from yours?

Which is best? I don't know – it depends on lots of factors. But having these seven – and I'm sure you could find seven more – helps you find one that works.

In fact, while we're talking about price, here's a question for you:

Do you think $2,000 is expensive?

I imagine you'd answer "I've no idea. It depends what I'm buying. It's a lot for a sandwich, but a pretty good price for a new Bentley."

Discussing price when you don't know what you're buying is meaningless. How can you know if it's a good deal or not?

It's the same when *you're* selling something that has a price to it. This means that, to reduce people's pricing objections, don't mention price until they're 100% clear what they're "buying".

Of course, they'll often ask "how much is it?" before you're ready to say. And, if you tell them early like this, they'll say it's too expensive and you'll have to overcome loads of needless objections. So instead say: "I've no idea yet. It depends what you want. Let me ask you a few quick questions so I can see how I can best help. Then I'll be able to tell you the exact cost."

A STEP-BY-STEP GUIDE, TO MAKE THIS EASY TO DO

1. Identify all their possible concerns – by asking them, asking others, using your experience and so on.
2. Think of 3–4 responses to each. Some people find a table helps them do this:

Their concern	Possible responses
	1 2 3 4
	1 2 3 4

3. Decide which 1–2 concerns you need to raise. These will be the ones you *know* they're most worried about. It's best not to do them all – "And the 71st thing you're no doubt dreading is . . .".
4. For those you do include, create your script using the four steps "introduce, state, remove, confirm".
5. Practice saying it, until it feels natural.

6. Rehearse your responses to the concerns you're *not* including, so you handle the Q&A well.

A FINAL THOUGHT

It can be hard to remove people's worries – as the young girl in Manchester Airport will testify – but you *must* do all you can to do so. It's the only way to get things sorted.

Build Your Snowball: Remove Someone's Concerns about What You're Planning to Do

The best way to do this is for you to raise the concern (don't wait for them to) by:

1. Introducing it – "You told me that…"
2. Stating it – "You're worried about X".
3. Removing it – "I've looked into this and we don't need to worry because Y".
4. Confirming it – "OK?"

This means you have to prepare by finding what their concerns are, thinking of a compelling response and practicing it, so you say it persuasively when it matters.

54

When you want to remove someone's final reason for saying "no"

My mum says "you know you're getting older when you bend down to tie your shoes and think 'what else can I do while I'm down here?'"

You see, there's always a positive if you look hard enough.

Which is good because life's full of people who love to say "The answer's no. Now what was your question?" Life is also full of people who are nearly convinced, but aren't quite. Both stop you moving forward with your plans.

One way around this – and you won't believe how easy this sounds, nor how often it works – is to simply include a negative in your question. For example:

"Can you think of a good reason why we *shouldn't* go ahead?"
So when they say "no", it means "no, there *aren't* any reasons why we *shouldn't*". In other words, "we should"!

In fact, there are only two possible answers they can give to "negative questions" like this. These, and the steps that follow, are:

Option	They respond	What happens next	Which means
1	No	You: Great. Let's get started. I'll kick things off by doing X.	
2	Yes	You: What's that? Them: I'm worried about X. You: [Remove their worries about X if you can] You: Any other reason why we *shouldn't* go ahead? Them: No (in which case, you start) or Yes (in which case, you remove their second concern, and so on).	It's worked

And doesn't this look oh-so-easy in a book?!

But, to be honest, it works pretty well in real life too, as long as you remember:

- When they say "no", they've said you can start. So, start.
- Build instant momentum by – *immediately* after they've agreed – say what you'll do, to get things moving.

"Negative questioning" works so well that it's important to use it with integrity. You're not looking to convince someone to do something they don't want to. Instead, you're helping them agree to something acceptable to them, which their "No Habit" might have prevented.

 Build Your Snowball: Remove Someone's Final Reason for Saying "No"

When you feel someone's going to say "no" to you, try asking a "negative question" – "Can you think of a good reason why we *shouldn't* go ahead?"

If they reply "no", in effect it's a "yes".

If they *do* give a reason why you shouldn't go ahead, work with them to remove their concern, then ask again.

55

When you want to get good outcomes from challenging conversations

When you're in an argument, have you ever noticed how the conversation can go round in circles?

A: You shouldn't have done X.
B: *Well I did.*
A: Yes, but you shouldn't.
B: *Yes, but I did. And you shouldn't have done Y.*
A: Yes, but I did.

Sound familiar?

What's happening here is that you're both trying to prove the other person's more "wrong". But, persuading someone they're wrong is *never* a good way to win an argument. They'll either defend themselves, or explain why you're "more wrong". No, proving they're "wrong" won't work. It's more important to find a solution, than it is to be right.

The key to a successful outcome is to be able to see things from their point of view as well as your own. In superhero films, the villains don't think that they're *villains* – they're just doing their thing. Similarly, when someone's annoying you, they're not doing it on purpose. They simply have their own views and perspectives – both perfectly justified in their eyes – which are shaping their actions.

So, to get good outcomes from challenging conversations, there are two main things to focus on:

1. **The future, not the past.** The key question is "How can we improve things?" not "What the hell were you thinking of?" Talking about the past can help uncover what caused the problem, but stay there too long and it

turns into the Blame Game. A good rule of thumb: solutions happen in the *future*, so spend most of your discussion there. The past is for reference, not residence.

2. **"We", not "you versus me".** Again, focus on "How will *we* improve things?" not "What the hell were *you* thinking of?"

Both of these are so fundamental to resolving conflict that I'll keep referring to them throughout this chapter.

A FOUR-STEP APPROACH TO RESOLVING CHALLENGING SITUATIONS

To ensure your conversation focuses on both "future" and "we", there are four key steps:

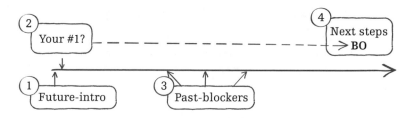

Step 1: Future-intro

Your first sentence sets the tone for the conversation. When you start by focusing on the future, the conversation is more likely to. When you don't, it won't.

The best approach is usually to acknowledge the past, then be clear that the conversation is future-focused. Two examples:

> *"It's fair to say neither of us would choose things to be as they are. So, let's identify ways we can take things forward, so we both feel more comfortable."; or*
>
> *"I don't think either of us enjoyed last week's meeting. I want to ensure that we both prefer next week's. Let's discuss how we can make sure we do."*

Both examples are future-focused (no Blame Game) and avoid the "you versus me". So, they incorporate the two critical elements:

☑ Future

☑ We

Step 2: Find their top priority ("Your #1?")

You've a better chance of persuading the other person if you:

- Know what's important to them; and
- Show how your proposed solution helps them get more of it

This makes it important to find their priorities straight away. So, immediately after your future-intro, your second sentence might be:

> *"I want to make sure we're focusing on the right things. So, what's your main priority with this?"; or*
>
> *"I want to make sure this conversation works for you. So, before we start, please can you tell me what your key focus is here?"*

When they tell you their answer, if appropriate:

- Dig deeper – "Why's that?" – to find their real drivers; and/or
- Write down their key priority, so they see it's important to you; and/or
- If you're thinking "I'm not sure our chat's going to achieve their main priority", don't say so yet. Instead, just ask "OK, so that's your first priority. What's your second?" (having two gives you more options later, as you'll see).

You can now lead the conversation. So, you can go straight to the future – "So, how can we improve things?"

Or, if you feel you need to discuss the past to find the cause (*not* to attribute blame), do so first, and then go to the future: "OK, so there are two things to discuss here. Firstly, to find why things went wrong. And secondly – and more importantly – what we can do to fix it?"

☑ Future

☑ We

Step 3: Past-blockers

Even if you start the conversation the right way, it's easy for them to drift back to discussing the past too much. It's OK to do this for a while, but you've got to get it back to the future.

You achieve this with past-blocking sentences, which always follow the same structure – "ACKNOWLEDGE *but* FUTURE":

"Thanks for your honesty. I didn't like it either. But we agreed it's important we move things forward for us both. So, let's now . . ."; or

"I know it was frustrating for you, and I'm sorry for my part in it. But we agreed our focus today is to see how we can improve things. So, let's now . . ."; or a simple alternative:

"So, what would make things better?"

☑ Future

☑ We

Step 4: Next steps (BO)

The conversation absolutely *must* end with a next step – one or both of you taking an action to move things forward. This ensures there's progress. It also moves the line in the sand, so your next conversation starts from a more positive place.

A great technique for securing their agreement is **BO**, which stands for:

- **B** – Benefits: why it's in their interest to progress things (link this to their #1 priority they identified in Step 2).
- **O** – Options: 2–3 next steps for them to choose between, to achieve this #1 priority. Giving them choices increases their likelihood of choosing one of them, since "Shall we do X?" could easily lead to a "No".

So, examples would be:

> *"You said earlier that your main priority was that you wanted to look forward to our future meetings. From our discussions, I think we have three choices for how we make this happen – X, Y and Z. Which do you prefer?", or*
>
> *"So, let's look at what we can do to help you feel part of our team again. I can see three good options here: X, Y and Z. Which do you think would work best?"*

(To read more about **BO**, see chapter 18.)

☑ Future

☑ We

HOW TO PREPARE FOR CHALLENGING CONVERSATIONS

Now that you know how you want the conversation to flow, it's just a question of preparing for it in the right way. This involves knowing your:

1.   Desired outcome following the conversation.
       You need to know this *before* you start, otherwise how do you know you've achieved it?
       Have a range of outcomes, because you're unlikely to get the one thing you want. Also, a range makes it easier for you to identify options for your **BO** at the end.
2.   Scripts for the four steps above:
       Your future-intro.
       The question you'll use to find their #1 priority.
       2–3 past-blockers, should you need them.
       How you'll introduce your "next steps" at the end.

And, of course, once you've prepped, have the conversation as soon as you can (the next chapter shows how to initiate it – something which can be daunting). These things rarely improve if you keep putting them off.

WITH CHALLENGING CONVERSATIONS, DOES FOLLOW-UP MATTER?

Yes. Of course it does.

To do it, simply fire off a quick email confirming what you've agreed (don't ask them to re-confirm in the email – they've already said "yes"). For example:

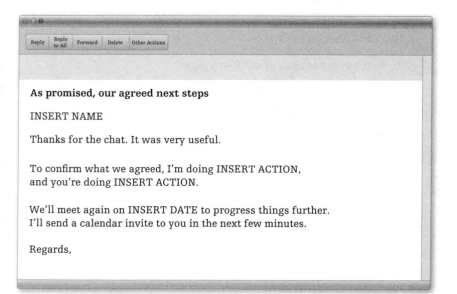

Reply | Reply to All | Forward | Delete | Other Actions

As promised, our agreed next steps

INSERT NAME

Thanks for the chat. It was very useful.

To confirm what we agreed, I'm doing INSERT ACTION,
and you're doing INSERT ACTION.

We'll meet again on INSERT DATE to progress things further.
I'll send a calendar invite to you in the next few minutes.

Regards,

Build Your Snowball: Get Good Outcomes from Challenging Conversations

There are two Guiding Rules and four steps.

The Guiding Rules:

1. Future, not past.
2. "We", not "You versus me".

Both Rules apply to each of the four steps:

1. Future-intro: set the scene – "We're focusing on the future".
2. "#1 thing?": find their key priority.
3. Past blockers: keep them future-focused by stopping them going back to the past.
4. Next steps: agree actions using BO (Benefit Options).

56

When you want to stop procrastinating about initiating challenging conversations

When I started writing this book, I asked my customers which of my techniques they find the most useful.

The most popular response was this chapter: how to start conversations you feel uncomfortable about, like:

- When you want to change how someone thinks of you.
- Revisiting a situation that went badly.
- Starting an important conversation that you know will be hard.
- Situations when you want to ask questions, but don't want to feel silly.

SERVE AND VOLLEY: HOW TO START AWKWARD CONVERSATIONS

Although these situations sound hard, the solution is actually quite simple. It's what I call my "serve and volley" technique. You serve an enticing opening sentence; they return your serve; and then you volley to keep the rally going.

To make this work, you need a great serve – an opening sentence that:

- Is intriguing and/or in the other person's interest for you to continue; and
- Stops early, so they say "tell me more" (their return of serve).

This means they've asked you for your Sentence Two (your volley), so *they* now want *you* to start the conversation you wanted to have in the first place. So, applying "serve and volley" to the earlier examples:

Want to change how someone thinks of you?

You: (Serve) I've been thinking, I'm not sure the way we work together brings you as much value as it could.

Them: (Return) What do you mean? (This is virtually the only response they could give)

You: (Volley) Well, it'd be better if . . . (and you're now discussing the topic you wanted to)

Want to revisit a situation that went badly?

You: (Serve) You taught me something invaluable the other day. Thank you.

Them: (Return) What was it? (Again, virtually their only possible response)

You: (Volley) Well, do you remember when X happened? I've been thinking about it since, and realize . . .

Want to start an important conversation that you know will be hard?

You: It's fair to say that neither of us enjoyed how X went. I have an idea about how I can rectify things.

Them: What is it? (Again, their only possible response)

You: Well, I thought that next time we could . . .

Choose your own sentences, of course. But if your Sentence One is good, they'll ask for your Sentence Two. So you've successfully started the conversation you felt uncomfortable about.

But what about the other example I gave earlier? The one where you want to ask questions but don't want to feel stupid? Well, this is one of my favourites; it works every time.

You serve with: "The last thing I want to do is bore you with irrelevant information. So, do you mind if I ask some questions?"

What could they possibly say in response? "No – be irrelevant"?!

Their only possible return is "What do you want to ask?", and you can comfortably volley your questions back over the net.

Build Your Snowball: Stop Procrastinating About Having Challenging Conversations

To address awkward conversations quickly, script and practice your Sentence One to make sure it:

- Is intriguing and/or in the other person's interest for you to continue; and
- Stops early, so they ask you to do so.

This means that *they're* requesting you have the conversation that you always wanted to have.

57

When you want to stop your messages becoming diluted

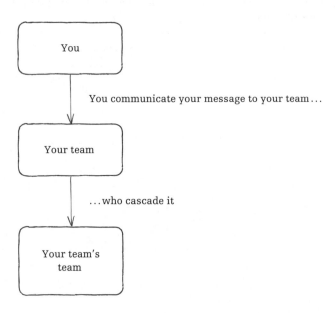

When leaders ask me to improve communication cascades within their company, I always ask two questions:

> Question 1: When your team cascades your messages, do they enhance them, add nothing or dilute them?
> They virtually all say "dilute".
> Question 2: And whose fault is that?
> Most say "my team's". The rest say "their teams'". And *nobody* says "mine".

This unearths two big problems:

- Answer 1 is, when you think about it, ridiculous. If your team enhances your message, it makes sense to cascade through them. If they don't, what's the point of going through them? Why not just skip the middle-man and communicate directly with their teams? But the fact that they actually dilute them – in other words, make them worse – makes this a terrible idea.
- Answer 2 raises an interesting point. In effect, people are saying "I choose to cascade my messages in a way I know dilutes them and makes things worse. And it's everyone else's fault but mine".

When people cascade *your* messages, it's *your* responsibility to help

I recently watched a TV programme where British Airways asked celebrity chef Heston Blumenthal to improve their in-flight food. He found that BA cooked food on land (where he said it tasted great), then transported it to the airplane, where the in-flight crew heated and served it (where he said it wasn't as nice).

He then said something I really liked: a chef's responsibility ends when the food arrives on the customer's table, not when it leaves the kitchen.

It's the same with cascading: it's *your responsibility* that your teams hear the right message to cascade. *Your responsibility* can't end when you create the cascade pack, add a covering email and press "send".

This means it's *your responsibility* to:

- Communicate your messages to them, in the same way you want them to cascade the messages onwards. So, you're going to have to make your communication interesting, probably verbal, face to face if possible, interactive, personalized to them, and so on. If you don't, but expect them to, it's like a parent with a mouth full of food telling their child "don't speak with food in your mouth".
- Give them very clear, very few messages that are easy to cascade. If you don't, it's too hard for them to do it well.
- Ensure they have the necessary skills, motivation and confidence to cascade. For example, you could train them, ask how you can help make it easy, suggest they read the next chapter *"When you want to stop diluting other people's messages"*.
- Set clear expectations about cascading. For instance, I imagine you don't want them to forward your messages "FYI" (but I bet some do).
- Ask for – and be open to – their feedback about cascades and how to improve them.

- Ask for – and be open to – their teams' feedback on how it feels to receive these cascaded messages.
- Vary your communications: sometimes PowerPoint, sometimes a document or conference call; change the agenda; when appropriate, skip a hierarchy level and communicate directly with everyone (this also helps your team see how you want it done).

You'll notice I used the words *"your responsibility"* a lot. That's because it is. A chef can't delegate responsibility for the quality of his customer's experience. And neither can you.

Build Your Snowball: Stop Your Messages Becoming Diluted

When you want people to cascade your messages, it's *your responsibility* to give them the ability, motivation, confidence and material to do it well.

This is going to take much more than creating a slide-set that you'd feel comfortable presenting, then sending it to them with no direction how to use it.

58

When you want to stop diluting other people's messages

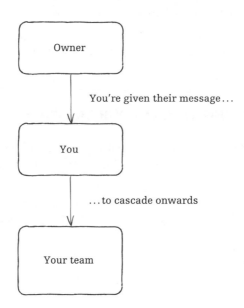

Owner

You're given their message...

You

...to cascade onwards

Your team

Cascading other people's messages is hard. You might:

- Have been given poor material.
- Have no time.
- Not agree with the message.
- Feel uncomfortable delivering it.
- Think it's not your job.

- Just not want to.
- Feel annoyed with your team that day, so don't want to talk to them about anything.
- Think the message is boring, pointless or "corporate drivel".
- Find it hard to *passionately* deliver someone else's words (I know I do).
- Think "there are just too many of these cascades".
- Expect these so-called "critical" messages to be superseded by Something More Important in the next few days.
- Feel unsupported by the owner.
- And so on . . .

I guess the length of this list shows I work on these things a lot. And that people have plenty of reasons to hate them!

If you recognize any of these, it'll be hard for you to cascade effectively, even if you want to. And, if you don't want to, that's a different book!

The previous chapter explained how it's the owner's responsibility to do all they can to help you cascade (maybe suggest your boss reads it?)

But it's also *your* responsibility to do all *you* can to enhance the message. After all, if you add nothing, there's no point in it coming through you. The owner might as well have gone directly to your team.

WHEN CASCADING, BE A COLOUR CAR WASH

Imagine a dull gray car going into a car wash, which uses paint instead of water. So, the car goes in boring, but comes out fascinating and multi-coloured.

When you're cascading, you're the Colour Car Wash. You get the gray raw material – the owner's messages – and turn it into something fascinating and multi-coloured for your team. The rest of this chapter will help you do this, by showing:

1. How to be a Colour Car Wash.
2. What to do when you can't.

HOW TO BE A COLOUR CAR WASH

The foundations of successful cascading are the same as for any communication, as I described in chapter 1:

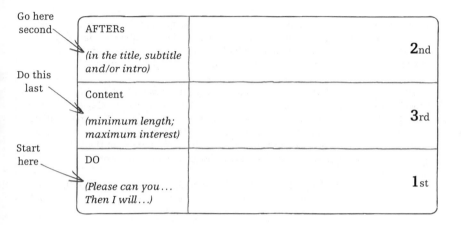

But, when you're cascading, it's also important to add your own slant to enhance the message. This makes your communication personal – it becomes *"yours"* in some way. This helps you bring passion and energy.

Four effective ways to personalize messages, along with examples I've seen work well are:

Technique	Example
Your emotions	"Our revenue target for this year is $2 billion. When I first saw this number, I felt intimidated, and – to be honest – not quite sure where to start. But then, as I looked into it more deeply, it became clear what we have to do".
Your experiences inside work (use the most interesting ones)	"Our new situation reminds me of when I first came here. The person who'd recruited me had just been suspended. Nobody seemed to know why I was there. Let's just say that my previous job was looking increasingly attractive..."
Your interesting experiences outside work	"When I was a teenager, my father was Chief Executive of Liverpool City Council – at the time, one of *the* big jobs in local government. Because I was a 'cool' teenager, I wasn't revising much for my exams. He told me 'nobody cares now that I once got nine great passes. But, if I hadn't once got them, I wouldn't have the job I've now. Now go and do some work.'" "And it's the same with us here. Next year, nobody will care that we once did the project we're about to do. But, if we don't do it well, we're not going to be where we need to be next year. So, here's what I propose..." (I know this exam example well, because it's one of mine! I can still picture Dad saying it, and how I felt when he did. It worked. I passed. And I now say the same thing to my children!).
A relevant story/analogy	"I know it's hard to stop doing a job you like, just to find time to do the paperwork. But, if we don't, it's like a waiter being so busy serving food that he hasn't the time to collect money from the people who've finished eating. Restaurants don't exist to serve food; they exist to earn money by serving food. It's the same with us, because..."

All four help you add colour.

And all are miles better than "FYI".

HOW TO CASCADE, WHEN YOU *CAN'T* ADD COLOUR

As you saw earlier, there are lots of reasons why you might feel you can't add colour – nervousness about presenting (the next chapter advises about this), poor material, no time and so on. When this happens, you've only got three options:

- Don't cascade it at all. Don't tell anyone you haven't. Just avoid it in every way.
- Cascade it half-heartedly/badly.
- Ask the owner for guidance.

You can tell that I think the last is best. After all, cascading is not 100% your responsibility and 0% the owners'. So, wherever possible, go to them and set the scene, sound keen and come clean:

Set the scene	"I'm about to cascade X".
Sound keen	"I want to do it well".
Come clean	"But I'm concerned about Y. What would you advise?" Or "If you were me, what would you do?" Or "Please can you help me?"

Build Your Snowball: Stop Diluting Other People's Messages

To cascade others' messages, be a Colour Car Wash: ensure the messages are more colourful and interesting after they've been through you (use your emotions, experiences and stories to do this).

If you don't feel able to add colour, ask the owner for guidance.

Just don't, whatever you do, send them "FYI".

59

When you want to stop hating presentations

Most people don't enjoy making presentations.

And, even if they do, they certainly don't enjoy most of the ones they have to see others deliver.

Sound like you? If so, it's important you stop hating giving them since, when you look uncomfortable, your audience suspects you lack confidence in what you're saying. This may make them doubt your competence and credibility . . . and all because of something as petty as not having eye-contact with them.

So, here are some simple ways to stop hating them.

1. ENSURE YOUR CONTENT IS INTERESTING

When you *know* your content will interest/help your audience, it's a real confidence-booster.

So, include content they want to hear – for instance, how your topic will help address their aims, hopes, concerns and so on. This will probably mean changing your content from what you'd planned, but it's well worth it.

2. ENSURE YOUR DELIVERY IS INTERESTING

Include at least 1–2 audience-friendly elements – interaction, stories, quizzes, humour, and the like. So, for example, rather than presenting "Here are my top 10 ideas for how we should improve", this would be much more popular:

1. Explain quickly why your team needs to improve.
2. Ask them to pair-off and identify a couple of ideas that would help.
3. Facilitate a chat about everyone's ideas.
4. Add 1–2 of your own.
5. Ask everyone to choose an action.
6. Ask everyone to share their action with the group.

None of these would take very long, but would trigger more buy-in, positivity and – most importantly – *action*. And, of course, it's much more likely to work than simply doing the traditional read-through of wordy slides.

It also helps keep it interesting for you. And it's less daunting because you don't have to talk as much.

3. REMEMBER YOUR CREDENTIALS

You're presenting for a reason – for example, your expertise on a topic, your reputation, the impact you can have on your audience, people want to know what's going on in your world etc.

So, focus on why you've a right to be there, not reasons why they'll doubt you.

When you think about it, no audience want to sit through a boring presentation. It's boring for them! So, they're on your side. They *want* you to be good.

4. KEEP IT SHORT

Review your content and, for each bit, ask "Keep/Bin/Appendix?"

- Keep – if it's critical, keep it in.
- Bin – if it's not needed, put it in the bin.
- Appendix – if it's useful background information, move to an Appendix.

I showed this approach to one of my customers. She used it on a 30-slide presentation, keeping 12, binning 9 and moving 9 to an Appendix. In other words, she removed the worst 60% of her presentation *in only five minutes*.

She felt much more confident and delivered a great presentation.

This is a very useful, streetwise, *quick* way of improving how you present.

5. EXPECT GOOD THINGS TO HAPPEN, AND THEY WILL

With presentations, as with anything, you often get what you expect.

So, if your overriding thought is "I'm dreading this. I hope I survive unscathed", the best you'll achieve is to survive unscathed.

But, if you think "I'm looking forward to sharing my ideas with them", it's much more likely to go well.

6. PRACTICE. A LOT

If an actress doesn't know her lines, she won't be able to concentrate on her performance. Instead of focusing on the scene and other actors, she'll be thinking "what's next?"

It's the same with presenting. Unless you've practiced enough, you're focusing too much on what you're about to say, rather than giving the audience your undivided attention.

7. WORK YOUR BODY

When you want to look confident (even if you're not), these are the five parts of your body to focus on.

Your body	Why it works	The simplest way to be good
Stand tall	This is a great way to look confident. World-class presenters like Barack Obama do this very well.	Focus on your head. If that's as high as possible, everything else will be.
Lock eyes	Looking at people transmits certainty; looking away transmits doubts.	For small groups, lock eyes with someone for 1–2 seconds, then move onto the next person. If you're nervous, look at their third eye. For large groups, split them into four quadrants. Look at the middle of each for a few seconds.
Lock chins	Your head angle has a surprisingly big impact: chin down, you look nervous; chin up, you look aloof.	You should be able to draw an imaginary line from your eyes to their eyes and a parallel line from your chin to their chin. You don't want your eyes locked, but chin pointing down or up.
Plant your feet	Presenters often think their hands betray nerves. And they can. Usually though, it's your feet that give the game away. Ever seen a presenter rocking or swaying? They don't look comfortable, do they?	Give yourself a firm base. Stand with your feet slightly wider apart than normal (gives you sideways balance), with 60% of your weight on the front of your feet (stops you falling backwards). If you get nervous now, simply walk a few paces to dispel energy and help your breathing. Then re-plant yourself (feet apart, 60/40 split) in a new place.
Have sensible hands	You want your hands to move (this brings energy) but not ridiculously so (this looks . . . well, ridiculous). If it helps, imagine you're a tree – your legs are the firm base and your arms/branches sway in the breeze.	Know your hands' default position – in other words, where they go when they're *not* moving. Usually, the best place is in front of you, either praying or lightly clasped together (watch reporters on the TV news tonight. They always do this, and it looks fine).

8. BUT DON'T BE "TOO CONFIDENT"

Although building confidence is important, some of the worst presentations I've seen were by people who "knew" they were brilliant – you know the type: the ones who give the impression you're lucky to hear them.

There's nothing wrong with you having butterflies . . . as long as they're flying in formation.

Build Your Snowball: Stop Hating Presentations

Seven ways to reduce your negative feelings about presentations are:

1. Ensure your content is interesting – if you know they'll enjoy it, you will too.
2. Ensure your delivery is interesting – include audience-friendly elements (humour etc).
3. Focus on why you've a right to be there; don't worry about why you shouldn't be.
4. Keep it short, using "Keep/Bin/Appendix".
5. Expect good things to happen, and they're more likely to.
6. Practice. A lot.
7. Work your body – high head, eye contact, chin contact, plant your feet and "sensible hands".

And, if you want to start actually *enjoying* them, look at chapters 34–38.

60

When you want to avoid people instantly doubting your credibility

Have you heard this phrase?

> *"When I see crumbs on the in-flight table, I think the wings are about to fall off."*

In other words, if the airline can't do something as basic as clean this airplane, I doubt they can do something as complex as fly it.

Similarly, with communication, the smallest crumb-like imperfections can cause big alarm bells to ring. For example:

Small crumbs...	...makes people think the wings will fall off
Documents containing factual errors	"If you can't get the basics right when you know I'm looking, what mistakes will you make when you think I'm not?"
Spelling mistakes	"So, you aren't careful enough to use Spellcheck. Now, let me think... do I feel safe investing millions of dollars in you and your idea?"
Grammatical mistakes	"If it's taken you 20 years to *still* not know when 'its' has an apostrophe, how long will it take for you to complete this project?"
Presentations outlining innovative solutions, accompanied by terrible slides	"I doubt you can deliver anything cutting-edge if your slides look like *that*."
Speaking to the wrong person	"If you haven't done enough homework to know that you should speak to me directly about this, and not go through Alan, what other glaring errors have you made?" (the next chapter shows an easy way to avoid this).
Sales and marketing material that focuses on the selling company, not the customer	"I'm doubting your sole focus is the customer, because you haven't mentioned one yet."
Presentations without a Call to Action	"If you don't know what you want me to do next, how do I know that *you* know what to do next?"

It's impossible to get everything right every time we communicate. But it's inexcusable not to spend a few extra minutes cleaning up the crumbs. So, always ask yourself:

1. Am I speaking directly to the person I need to? (the next chapter will help ensure you are).
2. Is everything – the content, visuals and delivery – as impressive as possible?
3. What will my audience think are my crumbs? How can I remove them?

It's important you do this. After all, for people to think you're good, you must communicate "good".

Build Your Snowball: Avoid People Instantly Doubting Your Credibility

Get the basics right – use Spellcheck, proofread your documents, ask somebody to review them for you, pretend you're the audience and think "What will they hate about this?" Then fix it.

61

When you want to stop wasting your time with people who can't make decisions

"My friend fancies you."

The teenagers' favourite chat-up line. And also one of the most useless. Because, as we all know, when you're looking for love with that special someone, asking your friend to ask on your behalf rarely works:

- Your "date" will wonder why you aren't asking.
- If you're not there, you can't react to what he says.
- Chinese Whispers means messages might be misinterpreted.
- Your chances of success depend on his relationship with your friend.

Let's face it: involve a middle-man and your chances plummet.

It's the same at work. When you want to influence projects, you must speak with the main decision maker directly, not indirectly through a middle-man. This involves three steps:

1. Find who they are.
2. Get in front of them; and
3. Say the right things to them.

Here's how to do all three.

STEP 1 – FINDING THE DECISION MAKER

Sometimes, it's obvious who the Decision Maker is. If it isn't, you'll have to ask such questions as:

Who's the ultimate Decision Maker?
Whose project is this?
Who's responsible for ensuring that this is a success?
Who's the key budget holder?
What's the approval process?
Who else do we have to consult with, to get sign-off?

Then, just as we discovered as teenagers, once we know who the Decision Maker is, we now go to them directly, not through someone else.

STEP 2 – GETTING IN FRONT OF THEM

Accessing Decision Makers can be easy. For example, if you know her, just call her.

When you *don't* know her, but feel you can approach her (or her PA) directly, say something like:

> *"Hi, my name's X, and I'm working on PROJECT X.*
>
> *"I want to help ensure it goes really well, so I'll need to know your objectives and priorities. When would be good for you, for us to chat it through?"*

This all sounds great, but what if you're currently talking to a middle-man?, If so, going straight to the Decision Maker could annoy the middle-man ("why are you side-lining me?") and/or the Decision Maker ("why have you contacted me? The middle-man's dealing with it").

In this situation, it's often best to work *with* the middle-man, not *around* them. This time, make sure you stress the benefits *to the middle-man* of you seeing the Decision Maker. For example:

> *"I'm looking forward to working on this with you. To help me contribute in a way that reflects well on us both, I'll need to speak with [DECISION MAKER] to understand her objectives and priorities.*
>
> *How would you propose we make this happen? Would you prefer we set up a three-way meeting, or shall I contact her directly? I'm relaxed either way – what do you think?"*

If the middle-man suggests you contact the Decision Maker directly, it's now safe for you to use the previous script.

If they'd prefer the three-way: *"Great. How soon can you do this, so we can get started?"*

Sometimes, despite everything, you just *can't* get in front of the Decision Maker. When this happens, decide whether you still want to be involved (I'd almost always choose not to be, but you might want/need to). And, if you *do* carry on, do all you can to find what the Decision Maker's most interested in, and make sure you all achieve it.

STEP 3 – SAYING THE RIGHT THING TO DECISION MAKERS

Now you're in front of them:

- Find their objectives and priorities. Knowing this ensures you focus on the right things.
- Agree how you'll feedback what you've achieved. This ensures they know it's been a success plus you enhance your reputation because you helped make it happen.

The best questions are the ones you'd expect. To find their objectives:

- What are your objectives?
- What outputs are you looking for?
- How will you know it's worked?

To find their priorities:

- What are your priorities?
- If we only achieve one thing, what must it be?
- If we did nothing, what would be your biggest concern?

To agree about feedback:

- How do you want me to feedback our successes?
- Who else do I need to update?
- How shall we debrief at the end?

These conversations work best when *they* do most of the talking (you're unlikely to learn much if you do). As the old saying goes:

"You have two ears and one mouth. Use them in that proportion."

The three steps in this chapter are simple to understand, pretty easy to do and produce great results for you. Imagine if you'd known this as a teenager.

Build Your Snowball: Stop Wasting Your Time with People Who Can't Make Decisions

The three steps to achieving this are:

1. Ask to find who the Decision Maker is.
2. Get in front of her, by going to her directly or working with your middle-man to make it happen. In both cases, stress the benefits to the Decision Maker /middle-man of you meeting her.
3. Then, find her objectives, priorities and when she wants updating ... and act on it.

62

When you want to prevent avoidable disasters

The *Titanic* sank about 100 years ago.

Imagine you'd been working for the shipping company White Star Line then, and were making your final preparations for the maiden voyage. All that excitement, pride and focus.

Sadly, in all the excitement about the positives, they didn't prioritize the negatives. After all, if the voyage had been a success, nobody would have celebrated there being lots of lifeboats.

Communication can be like this. When working on projects, strategies and initiatives, in all the excitement, people often forget to ask Lifeboat Questions, such as:

- Why won't this project be a success? *How should we communicate*, to ensure that it is?
- Which people will make or break this initiative? *How should we communicate*, to ensure they *make* it?
- Who might rebel against this strategy? *How should we communicate*, to pre-empt and remove their concerns?
- Which people are most worried about the outcome of this project? *How should we communicate* to reassure them, rather than wait until they start panicking?

When companies ask me to create communications to help initiatives succeed, my first questions always establish their desired outcome – *What do you want to achieve? How will you know you've done so?* And so on. People are usually pretty clear on their answers to these.

But my second questions always seek to establish what might go wrong – the Lifeboat Questions. This time, in response they usually say, "Good question. I haven't thought about that".

But it's *critical*. For instance, my asking these questions unearthed such information as:

- The Board member who realized her presentation about the year's new initiatives would have disengaged her already-overworked team.
- The company who realized that their new venture's success/failure depended on how assiduously their managers changed their habits and followed up. But their planning hadn't even considered these managers.
- The multinational company that realized the launch of its new service was going to antagonize virtually their entire salesforce, so much so that they wouldn't want to sell it.

Once you've identified potential problems, proactively eliminate them.

The weird thing with this is that, when things subsequently run smoothly, nobody celebrates the fact you averted disaster. It never even became an issue.

But, on balance, I've found that most people prefer to have enough Lifeboats.

Build Your Snowball: Prevent Avoidable Disasters

When planning, as well as focusing on the positives, remember to ask Lifeboat Questions – "What might go wrong, and how can we reduce the chances of this happening?"

Then, proactively communicate to minimize their likelihood and severity.

63

When you want to stop saying irrelevant stuff

During the past few years, many people have tried to sell me things that I don't want:

- Cars – I can't drive.
- Bad debt insurance – our customers pay in advance.
- 3D glasses – I'm blind in one eye.
- Haircuts – I'm bald.

They all had persuasive messages. For somebody else. But the right message to the wrong person is the wrong message:

> A company I know well has worked with some of the world's leading brands for many years.
>
> They recently pitched to help deliver a global, one-off, three-day event. Their key message was their uncanny ability to build long-lasting relationships.
>
> They lost the pitch.
>
> The reason? The customer said "our event only lasts three days. Your *long-term* relationships are irrelevant".
>
> Ouch.

YOUR BEST OPTION: *ASK*

As I've mentioned elsewhere, the best way to tailor messages is – wherever possible – to ask people what they want you to talk about. This sounds obvious, but happens too rarely. How many times have you sat in Planning Meetings, debating "Should we cover topic X or Y?", "Should we prepare material to leave behind? If so, what should we put in it?"

It's interesting they're called Planning Meetings. I think a better name is Guessing Meetings. So, instead of guessing – and probably being irrelevant – wherever possible, *ask*.

I have a teenage daughter, Megan. Consequently, I recently saw an interview with Zac Efron (apparently he used to star in something called *High School Musical*).

During the interview, the flirty interviewer asked "Zac, if you were to take me on a date, where would we go?" An interesting question to ask a millionaire movie star. He could've said *anything* – charter a private jet and fly wherever she wanted to go, invite her to the Oscars, get her the best seats at a sporting event . . .

But, he suggested none of these. Instead, he said:

"I don't know. What do you like doing?"

"Dining out."

"Well, in that case, I'd take you to your favourite restaurant."

Very nicely done. One simple question, and he was able to suggest exactly what she wanted.

ANOTHER GREAT OPTION: JOLT

Sometimes, of course, questioning isn't possible and/or doesn't work. Maybe you've never met the person; or they're too busy to see you. In this case, as well as doing your usual research, your best bet might be to JOLT them, where you use all the information you have about them to work out:

Judged – How are they measured?
Objectives – What are their personal goals?
Like doing – What are their hobbies?
Time – Are they short of time?

Once you know you're talking to a target-driven, competitive, time-poor, golf-obsessed salesman, it's much easier to tailor your messages accordingly. And, of course, if you can find areas of common interest, that's great for rapport building.

So, JOLT helps you tailor messages quickly. It sounds perfect, yes? Well, no. I've had one piece of negative feedback about it: it sounds so easy, that people think it's obvious. So they imagine – often wrongly – they can do it.

So, here's a quick exercise: JOLT three people you should know well:

Name	Judged	Objectives	Like doing	Time-poor
(e.g. your boss)				
(e.g. a colleague)				
(e.g. your #1 customer)				

If you completed all the boxes quickly and accurately, then JOLT is something you're naturally good at. If not, I guess you realized:

- It wasn't as easy as you imagined.
- The **O** and the **L** are hardest (they're more personal, so involve knowing someone well).
- It's really important: you *should* know this stuff (when you next get to speak with them, *ask*).

Asking and JOLTing help you be more relevant and, therefore, persuasive. You might not succeed as quickly as Zac Efron did. But, you've a much greater chance of doing so if you find out what people are most interested in, then talk about that.

 Build Your Snowball: Stop Saying Irrelevant Stuff

When you want to be persuasive, insightful, useful and *relevant*, make sure you focus on the right things:

- Wherever possible, ask people where they want you to focus; and/or
- JOLT them, so you know how they're **J**udged, their **O**bjectives, what they **L**ike doing and how **T**ime-poor they are.

64

When you want to break the pattern of hearing useful ideas, but doing nothing with them

How frustrating is *this*?

- You hear some great advice – maybe during a workshop, conference or meeting.
- You think "I'm definitely going to do that from now on".
- You get back to your desk and forgot to do it.

Or maybe you do change for a while, but then drift back to your old ways?

I guess you've done this before? *Everyone* has.

And it's a real problem. It stifles your progress. It can be frustrating. And it's extremely expensive, both for you (lost time and opportunities) and your business (who gets zero return on its expensive investment).

But imagine if you *did* embed great ideas every time you heard them. That could potentially be life-changing.

This chapter will help you do this. But it – like you – isn't helped by the Forcefield of Death: an invisible forcefield lurking in the doorway of every room where you hear useful advice.

This forcefield only kills one thing – your good intentions.

Even worse, it strikes in *seconds* – literally as you leave the room. You know what I mean here, I'm sure:

- You discover a new idea and think "This is going to change my life in so many ways".
- Then, just as you go through the Forcefield, the phone rings and you have something to deal with *right now*.
- Then, another issue needs your attention.
- Then you have to answer all the emails you received while you were learning new things.
- And at last, when you finally get time to apply the new advice . . . well, it doesn't seem quite so urgent now, does it?

The Forcefield will always try and get you – urgent things will always interfere with what you were planning to change. You can't help that. But you *can* help embed the great advice you hear, by:

- Giving yourself *detailed* actions which are easy to act on immediately. For example, "I must get more people to recommend me" isn't easy to apply. Whereas this is: "I must look through my list of contacts today, identify the three who like me best, call them, and use today's script to ask them to recommend me".
- Diarizing these detailed actions *before* you go through the Forcefield of Death – *before* you leave the room. If you don't, you'll have to remember to do it (you might well not) and/or fit it round your diary (that's just not going to happen).
- Identifying how you'll keep remembering to be "the new you" – weekly diary reminders, ask a colleague for support, ask your manager to include it in your appraisals, and so on.
- Pre-empt problems you'll have in embedding it, and work out *now* how to overcome them.

All these take a few minutes; and you'll need to do them *before* you get to the door, since that's where the Forcefield of Death is lurking, ready to pounce.

Remember:

1. Good intentions alone just aren't enough. It's impossible to do something if it doesn't pop into your head at the exact time it matters.
2. When others are learning from *you* (say, you're delivering a workshop or conference session), help them get past their Forcefield by asking them to do some of the ideas you just read: detailed actions, diary entries, and so on. Remember, your job isn't to *teach* stuff, it's to *cause* stuff.

A FINAL THOUGHT

This chapter contains some good tips that will help you. You know it will make a difference. You might even want to do something about it right now.

So your intentions are good.

The problem will be when you go through the door of the room you're in now. So, beat the Forcefield by doing something *now*. You know what might happen if you don't . . .

Build Your Snowball: Break the Pattern of Hearing Useful Ideas, but Doing Nothing with Them

The Forcefield of Death ruins learning. It's an invisible barrier that destroys your good intentions.

Help yourself and others get past it by giving crystal clear actions with deadlines, and/or diarizing first steps, recurring reminders, seeking support from colleagues/managers, and so on.

It's not your fault the Forcefield's there. But it's up to you to help yourself get past it.

Conclusion: Build your momentum

TO KEEP YOUR SNOWBALL ROLLING, JUST TURN RIGHT

We recently had a new shower installed at home. It's pretty similar to the old one, but the controls are now on the wall, not by the bath faucets. This means that, when I get into the bath, I have to turn right to switch the shower on, not left.

But for some reason, I just cannot remember to do this. I'm so in the habit of turning left that, every morning, I turn left. I immediately realize (yet again) the controls aren't there, then turn right.

I'm not sure why I keep forgetting. Maybe my brain's not woken up yet; maybe my poor eyesight means I don't see the controls, I don't know.

But I do know I'll crack it one day, because there are only so many times I can keep doing what I've always done (and keep getting instant feedback that it's now pointless) before my brain recalibrates.

And that's the potential challenge with this book . . .

You see, I've written it so it's as easy as possible for you to apply instantly. If you like, you "only" have to turn right to switch your shower on. The problem is, of course, that your brain is hardwired to turn left. You've been doing it for years.

As Andres Ericsson of Florida State University found from studying violinists and pianists, it takes 10,000 hours of purposeful practice to become an expert at something. And, you've already spent longer than this communicating in the way you do now. So, you're an expert at that approach, even if it's not the best way to do it.

Therefore, even if you're quicker on the uptake than me and turn right immediately (and I truly hope you are!), will you still be doing so next week? Next month? Next year?

One of the advantages I have with my shower is that it's impossible for me to keep doing the same thing. After all, there are no shower controls when I turn left. I have to change direction. But it isn't like that for you:

- Your next email could be good or bad.
- Your next presentation could be interesting and drive action, or a boring information swap.
- Your next Update Meeting could be a 10-minute "next steps" pit-stop or an hour-long series of tedious monologues.

So, here's my final advice to you: help yourself embed the techniques you've liked best. To help you, use an "external force" – don't just rely on your brain to remember – like:

- Subscribe to my weekly tips to reinforce this book's key messages – at www.andybounds.com/tips.
- Create regular reminders – in your diary, a new screensaver, a note by your desk, a new autosignature that says "What are the next steps?", and so on.
- Seek peer support – tell your colleagues/boss what you're looking to change and ask them to tell you when you forget.
- Hire a coach.
- Tell your manager you want to discuss improving your communication in your formal development targets.
- Use the templates in the Appendix.

Anything that helps you remember when it matters.

One final thought: people sometimes tell me they feel intimidated by the size of the task. They say things like "but this might take six months to change".

But, as I say to them:

- You're not saving time by not doing it. In six months' time, you're going to be six months older anyway. All that will happen by not doing it is that you'll become even more of an expert at your current style – the one you want to change. So, become better, not just older.
- Just choose 1–2 techniques and start with them. When they feel comfortable, move onto the next.

I cannot believe I keep forgetting to turn right with my shower. Just as you won't believe how you forget some of this book's techniques that you thought you'd always use.

But, imagine if you could embed them, such that every communication from now on was more impressive. Think of the time you'd save; all those "yeses" you'd get; the more fun you'd have; the less negatives you'd experience.

I've seen these techniques change the way thousands of people communicate, and the amazing benefits it's brought them.

Embedding them will help you build such a Momentum Snowball that you'll become unstoppable.

I know you can do this, and I wish you every success as you do.

                                                            Andy Bounds, January 2013

Appendix: Useful communication templates

TEMPLATE TO HELP YOU PREPARE ALL COMMUNICATIONS

Go here second → **AFTERs** *(in the title, subtitle and/or intro)*		**2**nd
Do this last → **Content** *(minimum length; maximum interest)*		**3**rd
Start here → **DO** *(Please can you... Then I will...)*		**1**st

TEMPLATE TO HELP YOU PREPARE BETTER PRESENTATIONS

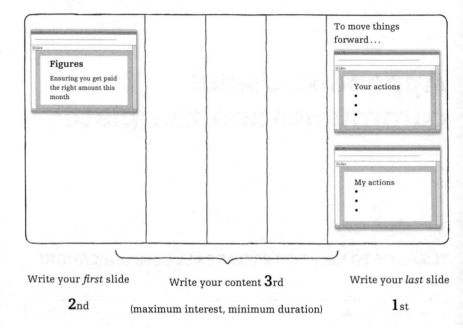

Write your *first* slide   Write your content **3**rd   Write your *last* slide

    2nd   (maximum interest, minimum duration)   **1**st

To help you remember
Create a blank presentation template with the above words on to remind you.

TEMPLATE TO HELP YOU PREPARE BETTER EMAILS

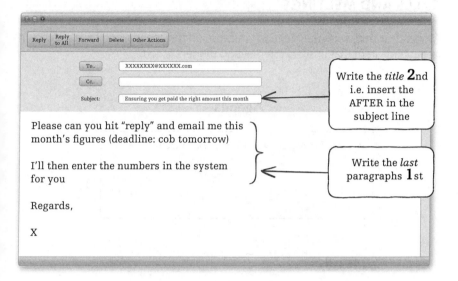

The **3**rd step is to write your interesting, short content.

To help you remember
Change your autosignature to:

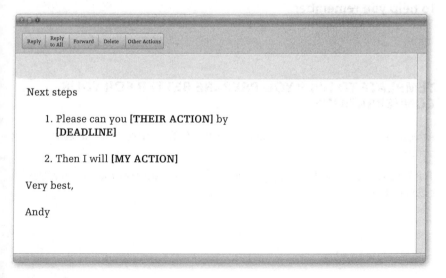

TEMPLATE TO HELP YOU PREPARE BETTER CONFERENCE CALLS AND MEETINGS

As your first step, write the meeting's purpose on the agenda, and have a standard last agenda item that ensures the meeting triggers *action*:

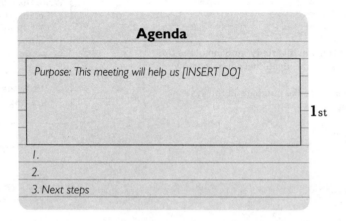

2nd, create an engaging title. Use it in your invitation to motivate people to attend.

3rd, create an interesting, short agenda.

To help you remember

Change your standard agenda template to include the "purpose box" and "next steps".

TEMPLATE TO HELP YOU PREPARE BETTER FOR YOUR CONVERSATIONS

As you'd expect, identify the DO first; then, the AFTER; then, your interesting, short content.

This is harder to embed because you don't have standard documents/templates for conversations. So . . .

To help you remember

Do some/all of:

- Weekly diary reminders – "Still doing 231?"
- Asking colleagues to pick you up if you forget.
- Adding "improve my communications" to your goals for the year.
- And so on.

Or – and this is more painful but pretty effective – when a communication hasn't worked, work out what was missing, and remember it next time.

TEMPLATE TO HELP YOU PREPARE BETTER DOCUMENTS

Firstly, identify what you want the recipient to do with the document. Then, write it in a prominent place. For example, when appropriate:

> To:
>
> From:
>
> Date:
>
> Subject:
>
> > **Action required**
> >
> > Please read, and then tell me which of Chapter 3's options you think we should pursue. My contact details are ___ _____.

1st

2nd, an engaging title.

3rd, interesting, short content.

To help you remember

Either add an "Action required box" to your standard template; and/or create a checklist to follow, something like:

Before	After
What action do I want the reader to take after they've read it?	Did they do it?
Why's it in their interest to do this action (i.e. the AFTER)?	Did they believe these AFTERs?
Have I made it... Interesting? (Yes/No) Short? (Yes/No)	Was it?
What are their biggest concerns likely to be?	Were they?
What can I say to minimize these concerns?	Did I?

To improve, next time I'll do...
More of... (i.e. what worked well)
Less of... (i.e. what didn't work as I'd have liked)

And for more help . . .

Does your company communicate well?

Does your team?

Do you?

Andy Bounds helps people achieve more every time they speak. He delivers this through some/all of the following:

- Consulting on communication projects, to ensure they work.
- Delivering conference keynotes, to improve the communication abilities of large groups.
- Upskilling and empowering leadership teams, to deliver improved communications and results.
- Helping sales teams sell more.
- Creating important communications that have to land in the right way.
- Developing communication guidelines that give people the skills, motivation and confidence to do things right, every time.

To discuss how Andy can help you communicate better, contact him on andy@andybounds.com

To sign up for his weekly communications tips, go to www.andybounds.com/tips

Andy's first book, international bestseller *The Jelly Effect*, is available at all major online and retail book stores.

Acknowledgments

I always used to wonder why books contained Acknowledgments sections. Surely, the author just wrote the book. I mean, how hard could it be?

The truth is, of course, very different. This book's been a real team effort, and I'm extremely grateful to everyone who helped make it happen.

The first person I want to thank is my editor, boss and – when she's not performing these two roles – wife, Em. All authors thank their better half; but Em's outdone herself. This year, while she's been supporting me writing this book, we've had builders working at our house for five months; been working flat-out on the business during our busiest ever year . . . and, throughout all this, she was pregnant with Tom.

Em, I don't know how you do it. I am – as ever – in awe of, extremely proud of, and very grateful to you. I just think you're great. And that's it.

Thanks also to the other Emma in my life: my wonderful PA. She's pretty much typed the whole book (ably helped by Vicky Etchells – thanks also to you, Vic). Emma has worked late at night and over weekends typing my originals, retyping my edits, further edits, yet more edits . . . Em: great work, great support, great patience!

The publishers Capstone have excelled themselves again, just as they did with my previous book *The Jelly Effect*. Thanks to Jenny, Tess, Megan, Holly, Iain: you and your colleagues have done a great job.

And finally, of course, thanks to my wonderful children . . .

Meg, you do your best to keep me trendy and hip. And I think we'd both agree it's working pretty well; especially when you play those top tracks from the Hit Parade. They sure have a great beat, don't they?

Jack, the worst moment in my life was when I could no longer beat you at any sport whatsoever. Sadly, this happened when you were about three.

Maia, thanks for teaching me Helly Pelly. I'll win one day . . . after we've finished colouring in our 125th picture of the morning.

And to our beautiful baby Tom: welcome to our family. We all love you so much. Thanks for waiting until the builders had finished before you popped out. Now, will you please go to sleep.

About Andy Bounds

Andy Bounds helps companies communicate better.

Credited by his customers with helping them generate £billions of value, Andy has helped people all over the world to achieve more every time they speak.

His book *The Jelly Effect* is an international bestseller. His successes led to him being awarded the title Britain's Sales Trainer of the Year.

To receive his Tuesday Tips – weekly hints and tips showing how to communicate better – visit www.andybounds.com/tips

Index